HENDERSON

MATT AND TOM OLDFIELD

ULTIMATE FOOTBALL HEROES

HENDERSON

FROM THE PLAYGROUND
TO THE PITCH

DINO

First published by Dino Books in 2022,
an imprint of Bonnier Books UK,
4th Floor, Victoria House, Bloomsbury Square, London WC1B 4DA
Owned by Bonnier Books,
Sveavägen 56, Stockholm, Sweden

🐦 @UFHbooks
🐦 @footieheroesbks
www.heroesfootball.com
www.bonnierbooks.co.uk

Paperback ISBN: 978 1 78946 524 2
E-book ISBN: 978 1 78946 525 9

British Library cataloguing-in-publication data:
A catalogue record for this book is available from the British Library.

Printed and bound in Great Britain by Clays Ltd, Elcograf S.p.A.

3 5 7 9 10 8 6 4 2

For all readers,
young and old(er)

Matt Oldfield is an accomplished writer and the editor-in-chief of football review site Of Pitch & Page. Tom Oldfield is a freelance sports writer and the author of biographies on Cristiano Ronaldo, Arsène Wenger and Rafael Nadal.

Cover illustration by Dan Leydon.
To learn more about Dan visit danleydon.com
To purchase his artwork visit etsy.com/shop/footynews
Or just follow him on Twitter @danleydon

TABLE OF CONTENTS

ACKNOWLEDGEMENTS

First of all, I'd like to thank everyone at Bonnier Books UK for supporting me throughout and for running the ever-expanding UFH ship so smoothly. Writing stories for the next generation of football fans is both an honour and a pleasure. Thanks also to my agent, Nick Walters, for helping to keep my dream job going, year after year.

Next up, an extra big cheer for all the teachers, booksellers and librarians who have championed these books, and, of course, for the readers. The success of this series is truly down to you.

Okay, onto friends and family. I wouldn't be writing this series if it wasn't for my brother Tom. I owe him so much and I'm very grateful for his belief in me as an author. I'm also very grateful to the rest of my family, especially Mel, Noah, Nico, and of course Mum and Dad. To my parents, I owe my biggest passions: football and books. They're a real inspiration for everything I do.

Pang, Will, Mills, Doug, Naomi, John, Charlie, Sam, Katy, Ben, Karen, Ana (and anyone else I forgot) – thanks for all the love and laughs, but sorry, no I won't be getting 'a real job' anytime soon!

And finally, I couldn't have done any of this without Iona's encouragement and understanding. Much love to you.

CHAPTER 1

PREMIER LEAGUE CHAMPIONS AT LAST!

22 July 2020

Today was the day. The wait was over. Jordan felt the butterflies in his stomach from the minute he sat up in bed.

'Jordan Henderson, Premier League champion,' he said to himself, with a smile, as he looked in the bathroom mirror and brushed his teeth. 'That's got a nice ring to it.'

The buzz was unavoidable. From the sports channels on TV to the morning newspaper to the car radio on his drive to Anfield, the day's number one story was that Liverpool would lift the Premier League trophy that afternoon, after the final home game of the season against Chelsea.

The prolonged 2019–20 season would live long in the memory for many reasons. On the pitch, Jordan had never played with so many talented teammates – Mo Salah and Sadio Mané, Trent Alexander-Arnold and Virgil van Dijk, all under the watchful eye of mastermind Jürgen Klopp. Off the pitch, the global health crisis had shut down the season temporarily, making this a totally unique year.

There was a party feel in the Liverpool dressing room as Jordan walked in. He was still recovering from a knee injury, but his 'Henderson 14' shirt hung in its usual spot. He would need his kit for the trophy presentation.

'How's the knee, Hendo?' Trent called as Jordan took off his headphones and sat down at his locker.

'Well, I don't think I could win a tackle just yet, but I should be able to climb the stairs to lift the trophy,' he replied, laughing.

Trent laughed too, then went silent for a moment. 'Imagine what today would be like with all the fans

here…' One consequence of the health crisis was
that all Premier League games were being played in
empty stadiums.

Jordan nodded sadly. That was the only part of the
title celebrations that stung. 'I know,' he said. 'The
fans have waited a long time for this. It's cruel that
no one can be here to see it. But there are going to be
parties all over the city tonight and no one can ever
take this away from them.'

The game itself was a blur. Liverpool would win
5–3 but Jordan found himself checking the scoreboard
regularly, counting down the minutes until the trophy
presentation. It was hard to sit still.

At last, the final whistle sounded, piercing the
silence around the stadium. Jordan walked onto the
pitch to join his teammates as they hugged and high-
fived. Behind him, up in Anfield's famous Kop end, he
could see the trophy preparations already underway.

After a quick stop in the dressing room to change
into his kit, Jordan took his place at the back of the
line as the players waited to be called up to receive
their medals. 'Whatever you do, don't drop the trophy,

skipper!' Mo called, grinning.

That was Jordan's worst nightmare. He reminded himself for the hundredth time to make sure he got a strong grip on the handles.

Out of the corner of his eye, he caught a glimpse of the trophy, with Liverpool legend Kenny Dalglish helping to carry it up into The Kop. Jordan felt a shiver of excitement run through his body.

Jordan had been part of the conversations for planning the presentation and loved the message it sent to the fans by lifting the trophy on The Kop: 'We're celebrating with you, even though you can't be here.'

One-by-one, the Liverpool players were called up over the Anfield loudspeakers.

'Allison!'

'Trent Alexander-Arnold!'

'Mo Salah!'

On and on it went until Jordan was the last player left. He checked his laces were tied and re-positioned the armband on his sleeve.

'Jordan Henderson!'

Jordan took a deep breath and walked out onto The Kop. Despite the music pumping around the stadium, it felt eerily quiet. But at the same time, he could still feel the fans' energy. He pictured all the Liverpool supporters glued to their televisions across the country.

He climbed the stairs up to the presentation area, hugging Kenny and then staring in awe at the Premier League trophy glistening on the table in front of him.

With his medal around his neck, Jordan took a step towards the trophy. To his left, he could see all of his teammates huddled together and already jumping up and down. He lifted the trophy off its stand and carefully carried it over.

'Championes, Championes, Olé! Olé! Olé!' came the chorus from the players and coaches, with Jürgen joining in the fun.

Jordan stepped into the middle of the group, paused a beat and then hoisted the trophy into the air. What a feeling! He was bursting with pride and joy as he watched his teammates each take a turn raising it to the sky.

As the players got ready to go on to their private party, Jürgen walked past and wrapped Jordan in a big hug. 'You deserve this moment,' he said. 'I couldn't be prouder of how you've led this team all year.'

Jürgen then called for quiet in the dressing room and waited as all eyes turned his way.

'Lads, this club has waited thirty years to be champions of England again.' He paused as Mo and Sadio started cheering and the rest of the players joined in. 'It was always going to take a special group of players like this to turn things around, and you've passed every test thrown at you this year. Now go and enjoy the celebrations!'

'Oh, one last thing...' Jürgen said as the players turned back to face him. Then he yelled: 'Liverpool are baaaaaack!', and everyone shouted even louder.

When Jordan walked out to the car park with Mo and Trent, he still had his medal in his hand. He didn't want to let it out of his sight just yet.

He turned it from side to side and let his mind wander back through the unforgettable moments that had led him to this point – first, the big games from this career-defining season, and then all the way back to the beginning of his football journey.

His career to date had been a wild ride and, as he stepped onto the team bus for the short drive to the party, the memories came flooding back.

CHAPTER 2

RED AND WHITE, RIGHT FROM THE START

With little Jordan napping in his cot, Liz Henderson sat down on the sofa for a quick cup of tea. It had been a busy day keeping her son happy after a sleepless night.

A few minutes later than usual, she heard her husband, Brian, arrive back from his shift at the police station. 'How are my two favourite people?' he called out.

'Shhhhh!' Liz whispered. 'In here.'

Brian tiptoed into the room, with a carrier bag in each hand and an apologetic look on his face.

'What's in the bags?' Liz asked.

'Oh, erm, just some bread and milk,' Brian

answered, looking at the ground. 'I'd better put them in the fridge.'

'Hang on,' Liz said. 'What about the other bag?'

Brian's cheeks went red. 'I should have known I'd never sneak it past you,' he said, with a little grin. 'I just thought it was time we got Jordan one of these.'

He threw the second bag gently onto the sofa next to Liz.

Liz opened the bag, glanced inside and then looked up at Brian. She rolled her eyes and laughed. 'Well, sure, every baby needs one of these well before their first birthday!'

She lifted a tiny red-and-white Sunderland home shirt out of the bag.

'You've got to admit, he's going to look great in this,' Brian said, hoping he had got Liz's approval.

'He really is,' she said. 'But it's going to look like a dress on him!' She put it next to one of Jordan's little T-shirts on the sofa. The Sunderland shirt was at least twice the size.

Later that week, Brian was scampering from room to room. He had a new idea – and it involved Jordan and the Sunderland shirt.

'Where's the camera?' he called to Liz.

'Check the drawer under the microwave,' she answered, carrying Jordan into the kitchen.

Brian pointed to the programme he had bought at the last Sunderland home game. It was open on a page which displayed photos of fans of all ages – mostly celebrating birthdays and anniversaries.

'What do you think about sending in a photo of Jordan in his Sunderland shirt?' he asked.

Liz paused, seeing the excitement all over her husband's face. How could she say no? 'Sure, let's give it a shot.'

Together, they put Jordan into the shirt, which hung down to his ankles. Liz tucked it and folded it until it didn't look quite so silly.

Brian took four or five photos and then brought the camera into the town centre to develop them. Clutching them excitedly, he put the photos into an envelope, along with a short note, and posted it to the Sunderland Football Club address shown in the programme.

When the next home game arrived, Brian asked his neighbour to pick up an extra programme. When he heard the programme drop through the letterbox onto the mat at the front door, he rushed to pick it up and flipped through to the photos page.

'Nope, not this time,' he called to Liz.

Later that month, Sunderland faced Arsenal at home. Brian knew another friend who would be at the game and he made the same request for an extra programme.

When it arrived, he opened it and there it was. Their photo. Brian grinned and raced through to the living room to show Liz.

Crouching down to where Jordan was lying on a playmat, Brian held up the programme to get his son's attention. Jordan crawled towards him, looked up at the photo of himself and smiled a big smile.

'Did you see that, Liz?' Brian called, turning to see his wife grinning too. He knew that Jordan had smiled with no real idea about what he was looking at... but maybe it still meant something?

'I've got a good feeling about this,' Brian said to

himself as he got up and put the programme on the table. 'Something tells me this is just the beginning of Jordan's love for Sunderland.'

Soon enough, Jordan's little bedroom was covered in red and white – a Sunderland ball, a team poster, a scarf. As he grew from baby to toddler to little boy, football (and Sunderland, in particular) was all around him.

CHAPTER 3

FULWELL JUNIORS

'I've asked a few friends about local youth teams, and they all say Fulwell is the best,' Brian explained to Jordan one Friday evening while they were tucking into a supper of fish and chips.

Jordan grinned. Ever since his dad had suggested checking out some of the junior teams in the area, the excitement had been building. Kickabouts with his friends at the park up the road were fun, but now Jordan wanted to be part of a real team, with a real kit and a real coach.

'I've got a number here for Coach Dipper at Fulwell Juniors so I'll give him a call tomorrow and see whether they're accepting new players,' Brian said.

'Try to find out more about how they run things there,' Liz added. 'Remember, Jordan is still only six years old. If they treat the boys like they're about to go into the Sunderland first team, that's not what we're looking for.'

'Ask them what colour their kit is too,' Jordan chimed in, grinning. 'I hope it's red and white!'

The next night, Brian and Liz called Coach Dipper. While his sister, Jody, slept, Jordan sneaked down to the top of the stairs, carrying his mini-Sunderland ball, and stayed as quiet as he could, so he could hear the conversation.

The first few minutes were muffled but then he heard his parents' voices more clearly. 'Okay, that's great,' he heard his mum say.

'What time does training start?' his dad added.

Jordan punched the air in celebration, losing his grip on the ball and watching it bump down the stairs. He put his hands over his mouth and stayed still.

'Well, he's supposed to be in bed but he's sitting on the stairs so he can listen in,' Liz suddenly said. Jordan felt his cheeks go red. He started to scramble up the stairs but gave up when he heard the kitchen door open below.

'Look who it is!' Brian said, smiling. 'That's so strange. I'm sure I saw him in bed fifteen minutes ago.'

Liz was laughing too. 'The boy is a magician! I'm sure if we go back into the kitchen again, he'll magically be back in bed and fast asleep. Right?'

Jordan nodded, with a grin. 'Can the magician just ask one question first?'

'Sure. Could it possibly be about Fulwell Juniors?'

Jordan nodded again. 'What did Coach Dipper say?'

'We're in luck! Fulwell have a couple of open spots and they train on Wednesday nights. He suggested that we bring you to training next week.'

Jordan wanted to shout and scream and dance around. But he decided that was unlikely to be popular at 9pm. Instead, he gave his parents a big thumbs up. 'Abracadabra!' he said, as he raced up to his bedroom.

The wait until Wednesday evening felt more like four weeks than four days. Finally, it was time. Jordan scooped up his backpack, which had a water bottle and a spare T-shirt inside, and followed his dad to the car. He felt some nerves mixing in with the excitement. What if the other boys were all too good for him? What if he embarrassed himself by missing an open goal?

Noticing the uneasy silence, Brian put on one of Jordan's favourite songs. 'Just relax,' he said, gently. 'The other boys will be football-mad just like you. It's only a training session – not much different than your games in the playground or at the park.'

That helped. As they arrived at the school gym, Jordan was grinning again and pictured himself scoring a few goals. Still, he let his dad do the talking when they got inside.

Coach Dipper spotted them immediately, put down a pile of cones and jogged over to say hello. 'You must be Jordan,' he said, shaking hands. 'Welcome to Fulwell Juniors. We'll get started in a few minutes but come and meet the other boys.'

Brian put his hand on Jordan's shoulder. 'Have fun, son.'

Coach Dipper led Jordan over to a group of five boys who were already passing a ball around in a circle.

'Lads, this is Jordan. He's going to be training with us today.'

The boys all smiled and waved. One of them walked over while still keeping one eye on the others and flicking a pass as he walked. 'Hi, I'm Michael,' he said. 'Join the circle next to me.'

After a few passes, Jordan felt at home. He was one of the fastest in the short sprints and his touch was mostly sharp in the passing drills.

To end the training session, Coach Dipper set up two mini pitches for 3-on-3 games. He put Jordan together with Michael and a tall, skinny boy called Liam. 'You're down that end,' Coach Dipper said, pointing. 'And you get to wear the lovely orange bibs too!'

Jordan felt like he belonged there already. The other boys were all really skilful, but so was he. When the 3-on-3 games began, Jordan decided it was time to show more of what he could do.

Michael slowly dribbled the ball forward. Jordan faked a run down the left wing, then spun back inside, calling for the pass. Michael slipped the ball through and started sprinting forward for the one-two.

Jordan was about to poke a pass in his direction but spotted two boys tracking Michael's run. Instinctively, he knew that meant Liam was unmarked. So he dummied the first pass, dipped his shoulder to create a little space and then zipped the ball through to Liam, who had a simple tap-in.

'Lovely pass, Jordan,' shouted Coach Dipper.

'I help you get settled at Fulwell and then you use me as a decoy?' Michael said, laughing.

Jordan laughed too.

'That was a quality move, though, mate,' Michael added, putting his arm round Jordan as they celebrated with Liam.

Then it was Liam's turn for the assist, exchanging passes with Michael then squaring the ball for Jordan to side-foot a shot into the net.

Goooooooooooooooooooaaaaaaaaaaaaaaaaalllllllllllllll llllllllllll!!!!!!!!!!!!!!!!!!!!

'The orange team is the team to beat tonight!' Coach Dipper called out.

As Jordan jogged back, he spotted his dad watching

at the window. His dad had the same kind of joy on his face as Jordan was feeling. At the same moment, they both signalled a thumbs up.

At the end of training, Coach Dipper called Jordan and Brian aside.

'That was an unbelievable session, Jordan,' he said. 'You fitted in immediately and we'd love to see you again next week. I've also got a registration form here. No pressure – but after seeing you play tonight, I don't want to risk another team snapping you up first.'

CHAPTER 4

SUNDERLAND SWOOP IN!

'Are we there yet?' Jordan asked, yawning. He had been asleep for the last hour and somehow they were still driving.

Brian laughed. 'Almost, sleeping beauty!'

Part of the Fulwell experience was playing in full-day tournaments across the north of England. It also meant a lot of time in the car.

As they turned into the car park, he spotted a couple of his Fulwell teammates. He waved through the window.

While Coach Dipper registered the team at the main tournament tent, Jordan passed the ball back and forth with Michael.

'This is the biggest tournament of the year,' Michael said. 'Did you see the trophies in the tent?'

Jordan nodded. He was already picturing taking one of those home later.

Brian appeared with the tournament programme and Jordan rushed over to see.

'We're in Group 3,' Brian said, pointing to page two.

Fulwell got off to a good start with wins against a green team and a red team and a draw against a black-and-white team. That was enough to top the group.

'Let's take it up another gear in the knockout rounds, boys,' Coach Dipper said, while Jordan and his teammates dug into a bag of orange slices.

The quarter-final pitted Fulwell against a yellow team that Jordan had seen celebrating a high-scoring win earlier on the pitch next to theirs. With the game still 0–0 inside the final five minutes, there were some tired legs on both teams – but not Jordan. He intercepted a pass in midfield and immediately knew where Michael would be making a run. Jordan kicked the ball forward down the left wing.

As Michael outran his marker, Jordan saw all the other yellow shirts racing across to cover. Rather than just admiring his pass, Jordan burst into a sprint and was suddenly unmarked on the edge of the box.

'Michael, square it,' he screamed, spreading out his arms as he ran.

Michael was surrounded but managed a quick turn to create room to slide the ball across.

Jordan took one touch to steady himself, then placed a shot into the bottom corner.

Goooooooooooooooooooaaaaaaaaaaaaaaaaalllllllllllllll lllllllllllll!!!!!!!!!!!!!!!!!!!!!

If he was honest, he had scuffed it and the goalkeeper probably should have saved it. But he didn't care as his teammates crowded around with hugs and high-fives.

'Brilliant!' Coach Dipper said, ruffling Jordan's hair. 'Most lads would have just left Michael on his own there.'

Fulwell cruised through the semi-final, winning 4–1 with Jordan setting up one of the goals. By his count (because he always kept a running tally of these kinds of things), it was his third assist of the tournament.

'One hurdle left,' Brian said, patting Jordan gently on the back as he polished off yet another bottle of water. 'Keep making your runs. A lot of these lads look exhausted.' He pointed to the purple-and-blue team who were trudging onto the pitch for the final.

Just as his dad had predicted, Jordan was a step quicker to every loose ball. He won tackles and headers, then made himself available for a pass.

When Liam burst forward on the right, Jordan rushed to support him. But Liam slipped as he tried to cut inside and now Jordan had to run his aching legs to get back to help the defence. He made up the ground and slid in to win the ball back.

Taking a quick look up the pitch, he could hear the Fulwell coaches urging him to attack. He dribbled forward, forcing a defender to hurry over. With a speedy stepover, he flew past. But now another purple-and-blue shirt was chasing him.

Jordan's brain was already working out the angles. The selfish options would be to take a long shot or try another trick. He wasn't going to choose either of those, but the defender didn't know that!

Jordan pulled back his right foot as if he was going to shoot. The defender was fooled for just long enough, lunging forward to block the path of a shot. Instead, Jordan picked that same moment to lay a pass to Michael.

Michael didn't even have to take a touch. The pass was perfect and he thumped an unstoppable curling shot into the net. On the Fulwell touchline, the coaches and parents screamed and jumped in the air. Michael ran off to celebrate, turning to point to Jordan. 'That was all you, pal! What a run!'

Fulwell survived a few late scares and, as the ball rolled out for a goal kick, the referee blew the final whistle. The boys rushed together in one big hug before shaking hands with the tearful purple-and-blue team.

As Jordan collected his trophy, kissed it and raised it in the air like he had seen professional footballers do so many times, he felt like he could do anything. This day couldn't get any better.

But he was wrong. It could! As he was taking off his shirt and put on a spare T-shirt from his bag, Jordan heard a man in a tracksuit start a conversation with his dad.

'Are you the dad of the Number 9?' the man asked.

Jordan saw his dad nod and shake hands. He pretended to sort things in his bag while he leaned in closer to listen.

'He was terrific today,' the man continued. 'I'm Anthony Smith and I do some scouting for Sunderland. We'd love to invite him up to the School of Excellence to train with our other young lads.'

Without even realising it, Jordan had stopped fiddling with his bag and had drifted over towards his dad.

'We train at the Charlie Hurley Centre and...' Anthony paused as Jordan suddenly appeared.

'And here's Jordan,' Brian said. Anthony reached forward and shook hands. 'Jordan, Anthony was just saying he enjoyed watching you today.'

'I really did,' Anthony said. 'You had some runs and passes that wouldn't look out of place in a much older age group – and I got tired just watching you run from box to box!'

Jordan laughed, then worried whether that was the right thing to do. He looked nervously at his dad.

'Well, I'll let you get home,' Anthony added, shaking hands again and then taking a sheet of paper from an envelope. 'Here are all the details for training and a couple of forms we'll need you to sign. It was great to meet you both.'

As Anthony wandered off towards the car park, Jordan didn't move. It was like he was frozen on the spot. He just looked up at his dad with shock and excitement in his eyes.

'Wow,' was all he could say.

'Wow is right!' Brian replied. 'I'm so proud of you, son. What a way to end an amazing day!'

Jordan walked slowly to the car with his dad's arm round his shoulders. He could hardly wait to see what would happen next.

CHAPTER 5

HANGING OUT WITH SUNDERLAND STARS

'Jordan! Quick!' Michael called. 'You've got to see this!'

Jordan rushed out of the changing room to see what had got his friend so excited.

'This better be good,' Jordan replied, with a smile. 'I haven't even gelled my hair yet.'

'Look! It's Quinn and Phillips!'

Sure enough, Niall Quinn and Kevin Phillips were walking past the big window on their way out to the Sunderland first team pitches.

Before Jordan had a chance to snap out of his starstruck state, they both looked over. He froze and gave a shy wave that he instantly regretted.

'Smooth, mate,' Michael replied, giggling uncontrollably.

Life at the School of Excellence was going well for Jordan. He had quickly settled in as one of the standout players in the Under 9s and Under 11s, and he was learning every session from his coach, Elliott Dickman.

The coaches had quickly found that it was hard to get Jordan to leave the pitch after training. One Tuesday, Elliott and Ged McNamee, head of the Sunderland Centre of Excellence, were on their way to the car park when they saw a small figure out on the pitch in the gloomy evening.

Sensing their confusion, Brian got out of the car and walked over. 'Don't worry,' he said, grinning. 'That's just Jordan getting in a few extra free kicks.'

'He's still here?' Elliott replied, with a shocked look. 'Training finished an hour ago.'

'Well, you know Jordan...' Brian said.

Elliott and Ged both nodded, then turned to walk over to see Jordan.

'Even Beckham takes a break sometimes!' Ged called out to Jordan, who was whipping a shot against the crossbar.

Jordan squinted and recognised the two men. He jogged over to get the ball. 'Last one, I promise,' he answered.

'You'll go far with this kind of attitude, Jordan,' Ged said, patting him on the shoulder. 'If dragging you off the pitch is the only trouble you give us, I'll take that any day.'

Jordan smiled. 'Coach Dickman said I should keep working on my left foot. So I thought I'd start tonight.'

As Jordan dribbled the ball back towards the car park, Elliott turned to Ged. 'He's having another great year.'

Ged nodded. 'Oh yes. We're keeping a close eye on Jordan as one for the future.'

The next week, Jordan was walking past the big pavilion at the Charlie Hurley Centre when he heard loud shouts and laughter coming from inside.

He went up the steps and peered through the door. A shiver of excitement ran through his body when he spotted six or seven of the Sunderland first team playing a game of head tennis on either side of a tennis net.

As Kevin Phillips missed a header in the back corner, another big cheer erupted. Now a couple more of the School of Excellence boys appeared next to Jordan, wondering the same thing that he had. He grinned as he watched their same open-mouthed reaction.

Suddenly the ball trickled out towards the door. Without thinking, Jordan stretched out his feet and flicked it back towards Niall Quinn.

'Thanks,' he said, turning to chip it back over the net. Then he paused. 'Do you lads want to join in?' he asked.

Jordan didn't know what to say. Was Niall definitely talking to him? He peered over his shoulder quickly to make sure there weren't some other first-teamers behind him. But all he saw was Jack and Martyn from the Under 11s.

'Erm, yes sure,' Jordan finally said, relieved that the other boys were following him in.

After a couple of minutes of staring around the pavilion within steps of his heroes, it felt strangely normal for him to be heading the ball around with Premier League footballers.

He jumped to reach one looping header, keeping the point alive for Kevin. Jordan almost lost his balance but steadied himself with a hand on the wall. 'Nice one!' Kevin shouted, creating a memory that Jordan would relive for friends and family again and again over the next few weeks.

This was what made Sunderland so special to Jordan. It felt like one big family from the youth teams to the pros and, for one afternoon at least, he had been part of the inner circle.

CHAPTER 6

TOUGH TIMES IN THE YOUTH TEAM

Jordan slumped down in a chair and stared out of the window. Today had been one of his worst training sessions of the year and, of course, it had to happen with all the coaches watching from the touchline.

Sensing his mood, his mum Liz tiptoed into the room and put a plate of his favourite biscuits on the table.

'I don't know if I'm going to make it at Sunderland,' Jordan said, without looking up. 'Scholarship contracts are being given out next month and I feel like I've fallen behind.'

Liz sat down next to Jordan. 'Listen, the Sunderland coaches have seen you play for years. A few bad games or training sessions aren't going to change their opinion of you.'

'Yeah, but I used to be one of the stars in the youth teams. I was the one testing myself against the older boys. Now I'm playing less and less, even in my own age group.'

Taking a deep breath, Liz gave her son a big hug, fighting back her tears. Unfortunately, there was some truth in what Jordan was saying. She and Brian had noticed the same things.

Seeing Jordan in such pain, Liz wanted to tell him that everything would turn out fine. But that wouldn't be fair. What if he didn't get a scholarship?

Jordan was clearly battling with that question too. 'All I've ever pictured is getting the scholarship to stay on at Sunderland after finishing my exams.' He paused, nervously scratching his knee. 'Football is all I know.'

Jordan was right to question whether he would be part of the group that moved forward to the next level at Sunderland – because Ged and the coaches were having the same debate.

'Look, we all know Jordan's attitude is spot on and

he's a dream to coach,' Ged said, wishing that this discussion wasn't so difficult. 'But he struggled this season and hasn't had the same spark. We've tried him in different positions and nothing has quite clicked.'

'This is a tough one because he gives us everything he's got,' one of the coaches replied. 'But you're right. His end product has slipped this year... and even last year, if I'm honest.'

'The growth spurt hasn't helped him either,' Ged added. 'I mean, he needed it to compete with other lads in midfield but I think he's still figuring out his body.'

While the Sunderland coaches began giving out contracts to some of the boys and releasing others, Ged took more time with the decision on Jordan.

But the waiting made it even worse. Jordan saw the joy on some of his friends' faces and the agony for others.

Finally, Brian got the call and they headed for Ged's office. It was the quietest car journey that Jordan could remember. His stomach was turning cartwheels and his mind was racing, imagining everything from the best-case scenario to the worst.

Sitting around a small table, Jordan could hardly look up at Ged. If he didn't make eye contact, maybe somehow it would stop Ged giving them any bad news.

'Thanks for all coming down here,' Ged began. 'As you know, Jordan is one of the most popular lads around here – not just with the other players but with the coaches and the staff too...'

Jordan held his breath. Please don't say 'but', he thought to himself.

'...but...'

Jordan winced.

'...this past year hasn't been one of his best. That can happen with lads his age, with growth spurts and the extra pressure. Through it all, though, Jordan's attitude has always been a shining example to the rest of the group.'

Ged paused and saw the tension in the room. Liz looked like she was about to cry.

'At the Under-18 level, strength and speed are even more important. Jordan has work to do there, but we believe that he can make that jump here at Sunderland. So we'd like to offer him a two-year scholarship.'

The tears arrived right on cue for Liz. Jordan, who had been pale with worry for most of the conversation, finally relaxed and let a big smile spread across his face.

'Thank you, Ged,' Jordan said, standing to shake hands. 'I won't let you down.'

Ged smiled. 'Congratulations, Jordan. Let's get the forms signed.' He reached over for an envelope on his desk and pulled out four sheets of paper.

Jordan took the pen and stared at the pages. He had feared this moment would never happen.

Out of the corner of his eye, he could see his dad getting into position for a photo. Well, more likely, hundreds of photos.

'Jordan, look up as you're signing,' Brian called.

Jordan gave Ged a look that he hoped said 'Sorry about my embarrassing parents', and then grinned for the photos.

Ged walked over towards Brian. 'Jordan was just saying he'd love a photo of the three of you as well,' he said, winking at Jordan.

Jordan laughed and shook his head. Now his face

said, 'Thanks for nothing!'

But given all the sleepless nights and nail-biting car journeys, a family photo was a small price to pay for the scholarship on the table in front of him.

CHAPTER 7

BALLY'S
BIG GAME HERO

'Switch on, lads,' called out Kevin Ball, manager of the
Sunderland Under 18s. 'Five minutes till showtime.'

Jordan had been with the Under 18s long enough
to know that when Bally told you to do something,
you did it. This level of discipline suited Jordan just
fine. He was willing to do whatever was asked, from
cleaning boots to sweeping the changing room to
being early for every meeting.

There was the familiar clatter of studs as Jordan and
his teammates went through their final routine.

'How are you doing, Jack?' Jordan asked quietly.
Jack Colback, another Sunderland midfielder and a
good friend, had been ill at the team hotel. Even now,

he looked a light shade of green.

'Not great,' Jack replied, shrugging. 'But I want to give it a go. I might just need you to do some of my running for me.'

'Don't I always?' Jordan shot back, with a wink.

The FA Youth Cup was the highlight on the Under-18s calendar – and Sunderland had reached the quarter-finals.

'Charlton are a good side and they move the ball well,' Bally explained, with all eyes fixed on him. 'But if we match their hunger and effort, our talent will do the rest. Play for each other, stick together and let's have some fun.'

Jordan joined in the cheers and high-fives, then followed his teammates out onto the pitch.

Bally had been right. Charlton were fired up and zipped passes around with confidence. Jordan spent more time chasing and closing down than he did on the ball. Martyn scored for Sunderland, but the game was locked at 1–1 inside the final five minutes.

But this was when Jordan's fitness was often a difference-maker for Sunderland. Despite all the lung-busting runs from penalty area to penalty area, he was still racing around in midfield.

As Jordan jogged back into position ready for a goal kick, he spotted Bally on the touchline next to him. Bally was gesturing for Jordan to keep pushing forward.

Jordan raced over to take a throw-in and Bally was there again. 'Look for that diagonal run,' he called. 'They're really tired. Make them track back and keep up with you.'

A long clearance sent Martyn through on goal in a shoulder-to-shoulder race with Charlton's best defender. By the time the looping ball bounced, Jordan was already sprinting up in support. The defender blocked Martyn's shot and it rebounded out to the edge of the penalty area.

Darting towards the ball, Jordan felt a burst of excitement. With a quick glance, he spotted the Charlton goalkeeper was still off his line after starting to rush out to deal with the long clearance. Jordan took one touch to cushion the ball and then lobbed a left-footed shot, hoping to chip it over the retreating keeper.

The rest seemed to happen in slow motion. The

shot arced up and up, then down. The keeper dived but he was too late as the ball dropped into the net. *2–1!*

Goooooooooooooooooooaaaaaaaaaaaaaaaalllllllllllll llllllllllll!!!!!!!!!!!!!!!!!!

Jordan raised his arms in the air and ran off towards the Sunderland substitutes. Halfway there, he jumped and punched the air. 'Get in!'

Bally was even running down the touchline now too, joining the pile of Sunderland players, with Jordan at the bottom of the heap.

It was the last kick of the game. The final whistle sounded and Jordan got buried in hugs all over again.

'Next time you boys are giving me stick about making you run extra laps, I'll remind you of tonight,' Bally said back in the dressing room, grinning at them all. 'We were all over them in the last ten minutes.'

Sunderland's FA Youth Cup run ended in the next round however, but Jordan would never forget that last-second winner.

In the meantime, Bally made sure none of the boys let their standard of play slip. Jordan kept up his end of the deal with total commitment to his football. He had come too far to throw it all away now.

CHAPTER 8

SHOWING OFF SKILLS ON TV

'Alright, so the crew from the *Soccer AM* TV show are going to be here to film the Skills Challenge later this week,' Bally said, as he and Ged sat down in the cafeteria. 'Nathan definitely wants to do it, but we need someone else to go head-to-head with him.'

Ged nodded. 'Let's ask the lads. There are three or four of them who might fancy it.'

But there was a long silence when Bally asked for a volunteer at the end of training.

'Well, I never thought I'd see you lads being shy in front of the cameras!' Bally added, laughing.

Then a voice piped up. 'I'll do it.'

Bally and Ged looked up in surprise and saw Jordan

with his hand up.

'That's the spirit, Jordan,' Bally said.

Nathan grinned. 'It's called Skills *Challenge*, isn't it? Beating Jordan won't be much of a challenge.'

'Oooooooooooooooooo,' murmured the rest of the Sunderland boys.

Jordan laughed too. 'That's big talk. We'll see.'

But Nathan was probably right. He was the most skilful player in the academy and spent every spare minute working on his flicks and tricks. Meanwhile, Jordan was more likely to be running laps after training.

But this week the laps would have to wait. Jordan spent the next few nights working on skills he could use for *Soccer AM*. He might not win against Nathan but he was determined not to be embarrassed. He loved watching *Soccer AM* on Saturday mornings and so many of his friends and family would eventually see this video.

As the cameras started rolling, Jordan tried to grin through the nerves. There would be three rounds – and he was up first.

He flicked the ball up for a few careful keepy-ups,

then whipped his leg over the ball in midair quickly enough to continue the keepy-ups. He did that again, and again, then gave Nathan a jokey stare.

Nathan matched him with his own keepy-ups, spinning in a circle before bringing the ball to a stop, perfectly balanced on his foot.

Now Jordan went for his second trick. He flicked the ball up and twisted his body to the side so he could trap it between his heel and his bum. Then he let it drop down and clipped it up with his other foot into more keepy-ups.

Nathan gave him an impressed nod, before pulling off a trick where he started with keepy-ups. Then he turned his foot to the side and let the ball bounce straight back up into more flicks.

Jordan had saved his best for last. He clipped the ball up, flipped it higher off his shirt and balanced it on the back of his neck. He finished by pinging it back to Nathan, then turning to show off the word 'Wow!' on the back of his shorts.

But Nathan had something even more special up his sleeve. As Jordan watched on with his teammates, all hopping with excitement, Nathan showed off a few flicks, trapped the ball between his legs and grabbed a skipping rope. He then whipped the skipping rope round and round, jumping over it each time with the ball still safely between his legs.

Even Jordan was smiling and clapping. The *Soccer AM* team stepped forward to congratulate them both and named Nathan the winner. They shook hands before the rest of the Sunderland players crowded round, screaming and cheering.

'That was one of the best Skills Challenge battles I've seen,' one of the camera crew said. 'Can't wait for everyone to see that on TV!'

As Bally watched from a distance, he couldn't help but smile. Jordan really was full of surprises. All the other lads had backed down from facing Nathan, but Jordan was fearless. That was quickly becoming his secret weapon, Bally thought, as he walked back to his office.

CHAPTER 9

FIRST TASTE OF THE BIG-TIME

'I know I sound like a child on Christmas morning, but I've got to tell someone, otherwise I'm going to explode!' Jordan said, speaking fast and needing to pause for a breath.

Michael laughed. They had kept in touch ever since their early Fulwell days and tried to speak every week.

'I'm going to be travelling with the Sunderland squad tonight for the game against Liverpool.'

'Nice one. I'm free this weekend so I'll try to swing by and see you.'

'Oh, don't worry about that. I'm probably not going to be playing, but just wanted to …

'No problem, I'd happily come and watch on the

touchline with you.'

Jordan laughed. 'Erm... I doubt they'll let you do that, pal.' He paused, then realised he had left out the most important detail. 'Oh, right, I should have started with this part. I'm travelling with the Sunderland first team for a Premier League game.'

'W... W... What? No way! Are you winding me up?'

Jordan laughed again. 'I'm not. I promise.'

'Congrats, pal. That's made my day! You better give me all the details... the hotel, the meals, who you sit next to... maybe you need an old friend to help carry your bag?'

'Actually, you're going to love this. I don't even have to carry my bag. It'll just get brought through to the dressing room when we arrive at the stadium.'

Michael laughed. 'You're big time now!'

Jordan was the first to arrive for the team bus – there was no way that he was going to be late! Wearing the Sunderland tracksuit felt even better than he expected. He sat quietly for most of the journey, partly in awe of the first-team players and partly because he wasn't sure what to say. He just looked on as the Sunderland regulars played card games and told jokes.

Even though Jordan knew that he wouldn't even be on the bench at Anfield, it was still exciting to be at all the team meetings and watch the way that the first team prepared for a Premier League game. Every little detail was taken care of – his meals, his kit, his boots.

He just tried to absorb as much of the experience as he could. He listened carefully to the game plan and read all the notes in the scouting report about Liverpool. This brief taste of Premier League action was the perfect motivation for Jordan for when he returned home for the rest of the reserve team season.

But it wasn't only his football that was putting Jordan in a good mood. He had met an amazing girl called Rebecca at a friend's party a few months ago and she was quickly becoming a big part of his life. It started off as a couple of dinners and a date at the local cinema, but now it felt like he had known her for years, not months.

'Welcome home!' Rebecca said, hugging Jordan as he walked through the door after the Liverpool trip.

'I want to hear all about it.'

She probably got more details than she needed as Jordan gave a minute-by-minute account, but she loved seeing the excitement in his eyes.

'Well, after all that, I'm just happy your head still fits through the door, Mr Premier League footballer,' she joked. 'Now that you're travelling with the first team, remind me to ask for a nicer birthday present.'

Jordan laughed. 'I really don't want any of this to change me. So far, I feel like most of my friends would say I'm the same Jordan that they've known since school. But set me straight if I start to sound too big-time!'

Rebecca smiled. 'I'll be the first to tell you!' she replied. 'But you should give yourself more credit. I don't think I've ever seen you bragging about being a footballer or acting like you're more important than other people.'

Jordan was quickly realising that Rebecca made everything better. Even the disappointment of a bad performance or heartbreaking loss faded, when she was there to cheer him up.

As he continued to give his all during training, he wasn't sure what the next few years would look like at Sunderland. But he did know that he wanted Rebecca to be by his side.

CHAPTER 10

SPEAKING UP

Jordan could hear the Gateshead players through the thin changing room walls. The music was blaring loud, accompanied by singing and cheering. After beating Premier League side Sunderland 2–0 in a preseason friendly, no-one could blame them.

As Jordan took off his socks and shin pads, he knew what was coming. So did the rest of the room.

Ever since Roy Keane had taken over as Sunderland boss, he had taken a close interest in youth and reserve team games. In a lot of ways, Jordan welcomed that. It gave him an extra buzz knowing that the first-team manager was keeping a watchful eye on his progress.

But on the downside, there were days like this one. Roy had picked a young squad to face Gateshead and they had flopped.

When the Sunderland bus arrived back at the training ground, Roy stood up at the front.

'Meeting room in five minutes,' he said firmly, then walked off before anyone could ask a question.

Inside, Jordan dropped his kit bag in the corner of the room with all the others and found himself a chair near the front. There was never any point in trying to hide at the back.

Sure enough, Roy appeared three minutes later and was immediately pacing at the front of the room.

'Let's talk again about what happened today,' he said. When no one answered, he continued. 'When you put on the Sunderland shirt, there's a responsibility to deliver a performance. I don't care whether it's a Premier League game, a Youth Cup game or a preseason game. Today was an embarrassment.'

Roy looked around the room, shaking his head.

'Do any of you young lads sitting here think you can get into my first team?' he asked. A couple of the youngsters on the far side of the room stared at the floor in silence.

Jordan understood why Roy was hammering them, but he wasn't going to let one bad game shake his confidence or impact his chances of being on Roy's radar. So he spoke up.

'Yeah, I do,' he said, trying to sound confident but not arrogant.

Roy turned and stared at Jordan. Jordan could feel his cheeks turning red, but he didn't look away. This was either the bravest thing he had ever done, or the stupidest. He would soon find out.

After a few more seconds, Roy nodded and moved on to the rest of the room. Jordan breathed out quietly and got a little pat on the back from one of the older players. Had he really just spoken up like that in front of Roy Keane, one of the scariest people in football?

That night, Jordan told the story proudly at home to anyone who would listen. But when he woke up the next morning, he still wondered whether Roy had been impressed or annoyed by what he had said. But Jordan soon got his answer when he was picked as a

MATT AND TOM OLDFIELD

substitute for the first team against Chelsea.

'What you said after the Gateshead game took a lot of guts,' Roy told him in the dressing room. 'That's the kind of character I want in my team. Keep putting in the hard work and you'll get opportunities.'

Jordan nodded. He was speechless for a second but recovered quickly. 'Thanks, boss.'

Facing Chelsea at Stamford Bridge proved to be a mismatch. As Jordan jogged up and down the touchline to stay warm, he saw Sunderland fall 3–0 behind before half-time. What a disaster! Back in the dressing room, Roy was fuming – and Jordan was glad not to be directly on the receiving end this time.

'We've got to get stuck in and show some pride in the second half!' Roy said, clapping his hands to create some urgency. 'El-Hadji and Jordan, you're going on for Martyn and Steed. Start warming up.'

Jordan gulped. At the age of eighteen, he was about to make his debut! He tried to stay as calm as possible, but his head was spinning. He nodded and rolled his neck from side to side, then followed El-Hadji back down the tunnel to pass the ball around on the pitch.

The second half was only slightly better for Sunderland. Jordan did what Roy had asked – he chased down players, won tackles and tried to be positive when he got the ball. But it was hard work against Frank Lampard and Deco. Standing next to them waiting for a goal kick, Jordan had to hide a smile. He was a Premier League footballer!

Roy shook Jordan's hand at the final whistle, but the dressing room and the trip home were quiet. A 5–0 loss meant a lot of work on the training ground next week. Jordan felt pretty confident that he was the only player on the bus who would choose to remember this game fondly. When no-one was listening, he had asked the kit man to put aside his 'Henderson 16' shirt and his boots so they could be added to his precious football collection.

Looking out of the window, Jordan couldn't wait to speak to his family and friends. Despite the result, today had been another big step in his football journey.

CHAPTER 11

LEARNING ON LOAN

Just as Jordan was starting to think about life in the Sunderland first team during the second half of the 2008–09 season, Roy resigned. That was tough news for Jordan to take. He had been starting to build a good relationship with Roy and would always be grateful for the opportunities he had given him.

Stand-in boss Ricky Sbragia called Jordan into his office one morning in January. 'You've got all the qualities to be a key player for this club for years to come,' Ricky explained. 'But the biggest thing you need right now is regular football to get stronger and add to your experience.'

Jordan nodded but he wasn't sure where this

conversation was heading.

'We've agreed a loan deal with Coventry City,' Ricky continued. 'You'll join them for a month and it could be extended for the rest of the season if you're getting steady playing time in midfield.'

Jordan wasn't sure how to react. Was this good news? Or was he being sent away? A long minute passed with an uneasy silence in the room.

'Look, this is a terrific opportunity,' Ricky said, sensing Jordan's confusion. 'They've got lots of experienced pros to learn from and you'll have the chance to play ninety minutes week in, week out. That's what will take your game to the next level.'

Jordan called his parents straight away and gave them the update. 'What do you think?' he asked.

'This is a great chance to prove yourself,' Brian said, choosing to see the positives. 'Trust the Sunderland coaches – they've always done the right thing for your development in the past. Focus on Coventry now. Just do all the same things you always do – show up early, work hard, be a good teammate and show you want to learn.'

Sure enough, Jordan was quickly a big hit at Coventry.

He got a warm welcome from manager Chris Coleman, who arranged a tour of the training ground and the stadium. Chris also introduced him to defender Marcus Hall.

'Marcus will help you get settled and meet the rest of the lads,' he said. 'If you've got any questions, he's your guy.'

Jordan tried not to look too nervous as Marcus introduced him to the squad in the pouring rain. He had watched some of the senior players like Clinton Morrison on TV for years and he was excited to get to know the younger lads too.

Marcus and Jordan were given green bibs, and they were joined by David Bell, a midfielder, and Leon Best, a striker. They passed the ball around in a circle while they waited for the coaches to set up the drills.

Jordan showed that he could do a little bit of everything. He was tireless in closing down the others in a keep-ball session, his technique was as good as anyone in the 2-on-2 drills and his range of passing wowed the coaches in the bigger games.

'You've done a really good job in training this week,' Marcus told him when they sat down for lunch in the cafeteria. 'I'm always curious when we bring a youngster on loan. Often you can see that they don't want to be here, or they think they're too good for this level. But you've been great.'

Jordan was thrown into the Coventry team and quickly worked out where the strikers liked to make their runs. By the time he was starting on the right wing away against Norwich, he was full of confidence. 'Get yourself in the box at every opportunity,' Chris had said back in the dressing room. 'We know you'll still have the legs to track back.'

Inside the first ten minutes, Jordan charged into the box twice, in case a cross from the left wing reached the back post. 'That's the run, Jordan!' Chris called.

Again, Coventry worked the ball out to the left wing. David skipped past one tackle and created room for a cross. Jordan was already on the move. He saw Leon making a run into the six-yard box, so he stayed a little deeper.

David's cutback pass angled across the face of the

penalty area and Jordan's eyes lit up. He steadied himself and drilled a first-time shot into the corner of the net. The goalkeeper had no chance.

Gooooooooooooooooooooaaaaaaaaaaaaaaaaalllllllllllllll llllllllllll!!!!!!!!!!!!!!!!!!!

Jordan had no celebration planned, so he just ran off towards the touchline and his teammates chased after him. Leon nearly knocked him over as he jumped on his back. 'You little beauty!' David yelled, wrapping him in a hug.

Jogging back to the halfway line, Jordan couldn't stop grinning. His first senior goal.

The next time the ball found its way out to Jordan on the right, the Norwich full back was right on his heels, pulling on his shirt. Jordan controlled the pass but was immediately tripped. This was the kind of rough treatment that Bally and Ged had prepared him for in the Sunderland youth system, and Jordan refused to back down from the physicality.

He lowered his shoulder into the full back in their next 50-50 tackle and grinned as he won the throw-in, knocking the defender backwards.

This Championship experience was giving Jordan exactly what he needed – and Coventry didn't hesitate to extend the loan deal. He had adjusted his game to handle the physicality of the full backs he was facing, with more decisive touches and better use of his body to shield the ball.

But after a thumping tackle a few weeks later, Jordan stayed down, holding his foot. He instantly knew that something was wrong. The physio helped him off the pitch and he hobbled over to the bench. 'I heard a crack,' he said, putting a hand over his face.

He took off his boot and held a big ice pack over his foot. Even the slightest touch with the ice pack caused a wave of sharp pain. By the end of the game, he needed two of the coaches to help him make the short walk back to the dressing room.

Tests confirmed Jordan's worst fears. He had broken a bone in his foot and would not be able to play again before the end of the season. It made more sense for him to return to Sunderland to continue his recovery, so he packed up his belongings and said goodbye to the rest of the Coventry players.

'I know I've only been here for a few months but I'm really sad to be leaving,' he told them. 'Good luck for the rest of the season. I'll be cheering you on.'

But Jordan knew he was returning to Sunderland as a far more complete player after his thirteen games for Coventry. He couldn't wait to get back on the pitch. With Steve Bruce now in charge at Sunderland, it was time for Jordan to stake his claim as a member of the first team.

CHAPTER 12

BLOSSOMING WITH BRUCE

Back at Sunderland and fully recovered from his foot injury, Jordan was flying in preseason. His touch was sharp, his shooting had improved over the summer period, and he was always at the front of the pack on the long laps round the pitch. While some of his teammates were clearly using preseason to get back into game shape, Jordan stood out as the best player in every session.

Steve Bruce called Jordan aside during a morning water break. 'Keep doing what you're doing,' he said. 'We can all see the work you've put in since you went on loan to Coventry. Just know that you're going to have a big part to play for us this season.'

'Thanks, boss,' Jordan replied, unable to stop a big smile spreading across his face. 'I really feel like this is going to be my best year yet.'

Steve's words of encouragement left Jordan buzzing. In the next session, he cushioned a pass from Darren Bent, dribbled past Andy Reid and drilled a low shot into the bottom corner.

'Settle down, Hendo!' shouted Andy, laughing. 'Save those for the real games.'

Without anyone needing to say a word, it was clear that Jordan's teammates saw him differently now too. They threw the ball to him for free kicks and he was always the first option for defenders looking to play the ball out from the back.

When the first game of the 2009–10 season arrived, Steve had no hesitation. 'Jordan, you're starting on the right. Use the width as much as you can, but if we're not getting the ball out to you enough, tuck in and play more centrally.'

Walking out at the Stadium of Light, Jordan took a minute to look around the packed stadium and soak up the cheers from the sea of red-and-white shirts.

Not so long ago, he was one of those fans roaring on the team.

Jordan was an instant fan favourite. Even when he made mistakes with his passing or dribbling, the fans could see the effort he was putting in. It didn't take long for him to earn his own chant:

'One defender, two defenders, three
defenders, four,
Gets the ball, beats them all, you know
we're going to score,
Henderson, tra la la la, Henderson,
tra la la la!!!'

Ahead of a trip to face Manchester City, Jordan was hitting the ball as well as ever in training – right foot, left foot, it didn't matter.

'Everything was flying into the net today,' he told Rebecca. 'If I keep this up, I could get ten goals this season.'

Rebecca smiled. 'Well, I'll look forward to your goal celebration this weekend then,' she said. 'It's about time

MATT AND TOM OLDFIELD

the rest of the country got to see your dance moves.'

Jordan was somewhat regretting his confidence when Sunderland fell behind 2–0 against City. This was a chance for the team to test themselves against a star-studded City squad featuring Carlos Tevez and Roque Santa Cruz. So far, they were failing.

But Sunderland pulled a goal back, then won a corner on the left. As usual, Jordan let the big defenders attack the ball and hovered near the edge of the box in case a clearing header dropped to him.

After a scramble in the box, the ball spun loose, and Jordan was the first to react. He didn't waste time with a touch to control the ball. He just lashed in a first-time shot that flew through the goalkeeper's gloves and into the roof of the net.

Goooooooooooooooooooaaaaaaaaaaaaaaaaaalllllllllllllll llllllllllll!!!!!!!!!!!!!!!!!!!!

What a moment! Jordan's first Sunderland goal – and suddenly it was 2–2.

It was all such a blur that he totally forgot about a goal celebration – he just raced off, shouting 'Come on, lads!'

77

City went 3–2 up, but Jordan knew there was a way back. They had just recovered from two goals down. Sunderland got the ball down the right and Jordan saw space in behind the defence. He made the run, pointing for where he wanted the pass. The ball was slipped through and Jordan had room to burst forward.

He looked up and saw Kenwyne Jones darting towards the near post. Jordan fired over the perfect cross and Kenwyne thumped a header into the back of the net. 3–3.

'Yes!' Jordan screamed, rushing over to celebrate.

'What a cross!' Kenwyne shouted back. 'I didn't even have to move – I just let it hit my head.'

A City winner took some of the shine off the afternoon, but Jordan had been one of the best players on the pitch against a top Premier League side.

Seeing the disappointment all over his face, Steve stopped him on his way off the pitch. 'You were magic out there today,' Steve said, putting an arm round Jordan's shoulders. 'You didn't deserve to finish on the losing team.'

There were ups and downs over the rest of Jordan's

first full season in the senior side, but his potential was clear. It was one of the simplest decisions of the year for Bruce and Sunderland to offer him a new five-year contract in April – and one of Jordan's simplest decisions to sign it.

CHAPTER 13

ENGLAND EXCITEMENT

'I remember when you would run through the house pretending to play for England,' Jody teased as Jordan prepared for a key playoff game with the England Under-21s against Romania. 'It must be even easier without the risk of breaking a vase or a window!'

It had been a thrill for Jordan every time he represented England's youth teams. He had already played for the Under-19s, but the Under-21s felt different. He only had to glance around the dressing room to see the level of talent.

Manager Stuart Pearce gave the team a few final instructions, using the big whiteboard on the far wall. The players sat down to put on their boots and shin pads while they listened.

'Enjoy it tonight, boys,' Stuart said. 'It should be a great atmosphere and the fans will get behind you. Just keep your cool and play your football.'

'I fancy a goal tonight,' Jordan whispered to Phil Jones. 'A long-ranger, a tap-in, whatever. I'll take it.'

Jordan almost got one early, pouncing on a loose ball and unleashing a fierce shot that the Romania keeper tipped over the bar.

In the second half, he dropped to the edge of the box for another England corner. He saw the Romania keeper punch the ball away and immediately knew it was coming to him. But the ball took forever to come out of the sky. He watched it all the way onto his foot and fired a volley back through the crowd.

As soon as it left his boot, he felt it had a chance. It dipped just in front of the keeper and slipped past his dive, settling in the bottom corner.

Goooooooooooooooooooooaaaaaaaaaaaaaaaallllllllllllll llllllllllll!!!!!!!!!!!!!!!!!!!

The game ended in a 2–1 England win and a big ovation from the home fans. What Jordan didn't know was that there was a special guest at Carrow Road that night – England manager Fabio Capello, who was keeping an eye on the next crop of players likely to be pushing for a spot in the senior squad.

A few weeks later, Jordan was expecting to join up with the Under-21s again for a friendly against Germany. Then one phone call turned his plans upside down.

While taking a rare break to sit on the sofa and watch TV, his phone buzzed. He turned down the volume on the TV and answered it.

'Hi, Jordan,' said a voice. 'It's Fabio Capello.'

Jordan sat up in shock. Capello was calling him? Surely this couldn't be a wind-up from one of his mates.

'Hi,' he finally managed to say. Should he call him Fabio? Mr. Capello?

'Jordan, I'm using the friendly against France to give some of the younger players a shot and you're going to be in that squad. You had a great night against Romania for the Under-21s and you've been playing really well for Sunderland.'

Jordan was relieved that this was a phone call, and

not an in-person meeting or a video call, because he was sure his face had first looked frozen in surprise before dissolving into a silly grin. 'Wow, thank you,' he said. 'That's a great honour. I can't wait!'

'Congratulations, Jordan. We'll be announcing the squad later today.'

For the next ten minutes, Jordan just sat there on the sofa, with his phone still in his hand. The England senior team? He was still adjusting to life in the Premier League with Sunderland and now he was going to be sharing the training pitch with Steven Gerrard and Rio Ferdinand.

It was all happening so fast that Jordan just picked up his jacket and went to walk around the back garden. Maybe some fresh air would help, but his legs felt like jelly.

Finally his mind stopped racing and he started making some calls – to his parents, Jody, a few friends. He made them all promise not to say anything to anyone until the squad was officially announced. The last thing he wanted was for the news to leak out early to the press.

'I'm so proud of you!' Liz said, sobbing on the phone.

Once the news was out, Jordan's phone was buzzing non-stop. There was a special cake for him in the Sunderland cafeteria and Steve was there to shake his hand as soon as he arrived for training the next day.

'It's always nice to see hard work being rewarded,' Steve said. 'Anyone who has seen the way you play and train knows that you really deserve this.'

Excitement soon turned to nerves as Jordan packed his bag to meet up with the England squad. What would he say around experienced international stars? It would be crushing if he was rubbish in training.

'Look at the other names in the squad,' his dad reminded him. 'You're not the only young lad being thrown into this. There's Theo Walcott and James Milner. There's Micah Richards and Chris Smalling – they've been playing with you in the Under-21s and I'm sure they'll be glad to see you.'

His dad was right. There would be lots of familiar faces. Now he just had to show that he belonged.

Once Jordan arrived, he was relieved about how normal it all felt. He picked up a plate of food and sat with Micah and Chris. They swapped stories about their calls from Capello and all the celebrations their families had planned.

Jordan had just taken a mouthful of pasta when he turned to see Rio Ferdinand walking over.

'Welcome, lads,' Rio said. 'I can still remember my first call-up to the England squad. It's a lot to take in all at once but enjoy it. Don't put too much pressure on yourselves.'

Jordan nodded while trying to quickly swallow the pasta. 'Any other advice for us?' he asked. 'Like, stuff to know for training sessions, or things that Capello is really strict about?'

Rio paused for a minute. 'The boss just expects us to be professional...' he began.

Jordan could now see Steven Gerrard walking over to their table. Suddenly, he felt even more shy.

Rio had spotted him too. But he continued: '...and in terms of advice, I'd just say try not to be on Stevie's team in the mini games. He never passes.'

Stevie laughed. 'Yeah whatever, Rio.' Turning to Jordan, Micah and Chris, he added, 'He never takes losing very well.'

Stevie walked round the table to shake hands with all three of them. After a season of Premier League games with Sunderland, Jordan had mostly got past the point of being starstruck around big-name stars – but Gerrard had always been one of his favourite players. Now the man himself was standing in front of him and telling Jordan to call him 'Stevie'.

Jordan even surprised himself with his performances in training. His worst fear was turning up and freezing in the spotlight, but he managed to turn that into extra focus. He had nothing to lose so he just tried to play with freedom.

'Well done, Jordan,' Capello said as the final training session ended. 'Very strong week. You'll be involved on Wednesday.'

Still, looking around the meeting room, there were so many other youngsters with more experience than him – and 'involved' could just mean a few minutes as a substitute.

The room went quiet as Capello walked in holding a sheet of paper. He started reading out the names for the starting line-up. When Capello got to the midfield, Jordan tried to look relaxed, but he could feel himself sweating.

'Gareth, on the left. James, on the right. Stevie and Jordan in the middle.'

Jordan's heart started beating faster and faster. He was starting!

As Jordan looked over to the other side of the room, he saw Stevie wink and give him a thumbs up.

After the meeting, he rushed back to his room as fast as he could. His dad was going to love this!

'Dad, I'm not just starting... I'm starting in midfield next to Steven Gerrard!' he whispered excitedly.

Brian laughed. 'What a fairy-tale week!'

'That's exactly how it feels... and I don't want anyone to wake me up from it!'

That night, Jordan was wide awake. He tried watching some TV, listening to music and reading a magazine. But nothing worked. His mind kept coming back to his debut – picturing what it would be like to play at this level. He knew France were planning to play some of their youngsters too, but most of them were still big names. What if senior international football was a step too far, too soon?

Finally, Jordan drifted off to sleep and got enough rest so that he felt fresh the next morning. He bounced out of bed and could feel the nervous energy building already.

By kick-off, he was desperate to get stuck in. Capello and the coaches had gone through the game plan and explained how they wanted him to work with Stevie in midfield. Standing in the tunnel, Jordan grinned and felt himself relax a little. This moment – his full international debut for England – was something he would tell his children and grandchildren about some day. Whatever happened, he was going to enjoy it.

'Good luck, tonight,' Stevie said on his way to the front of the line. 'Let's boss it together in midfield.'

The roar from the Wembley crowd sent a tingle down Jordan's spine. He looked over to the far side of the stadium, knowing that his family were there somewhere to cheer him on.

But the game slipped away from England – they

lost 2–1. It wasn't Jordan's best game, but it certainly wasn't his worst either. For all his running, he struggled to get on the ball in the right areas.

'Son, remember you're still only twenty,' Brian pointed out, reacting to the disappointment in Jordan's voice after the game. 'If I'd told you a year ago that you'd be playing for Capello, you'd have rolled around laughing. This is just another part of the journey.'

Jordan nodded. As usual, he was being his own toughest critic when it came to assessing his performances. All in all, it had been an incredible week that had taken his game to another level.

CHAPTER 14

LIVERPOOL COME CALLING

After a long season capped by winning Sunderland's Young Player of the Year award, Jordan had seen and played enough football for one year. He and Rebecca booked a few weeks away in the sun and began packing a suitcase.

Meanwhile, an hour away in Liverpool, important meetings were taking place ahead of a busy summer in the transfer market. Little did Jordan know that his name was coming up a lot.

'Next season has to be better because we're getting left behind,' coach Damien Comolli said. 'You know the fans are feeling it after Manchester United won the league again.'

'We need fresher legs in midfield,' one director insisted. 'That means taking some of the pressure off Stevie. Jordan Henderson at Sunderland looks like one for the future.'

'He never stops running,' added another. 'He could be the spark we're looking for.'

'Okay, but let's not forget that he's still really young,' said a fourth voice. 'Can he handle the pressure? We need big names if we're going to turn things around here.'

'But he could be one piece of the puzzle,' explained Damien. 'He's the kind of player that could be a bridge between the current squad and our future side.'

Even on holiday, Jordan heard the rumours about transfer bids from some of the Premier League's biggest clubs. He tried to block out the noise, though it was still flattering to be linked with those kinds of teams.

'If it happens, it would be an incredible opportunity,' he said calmly when Rebecca asked him about what he hoped would happen. 'But I'm happy at Sunderland so let's wait and see. I just hope this doesn't drag on all summer. I don't want to be checking my phone every ten minutes.'

Luckily, he soon got his wish, and the situation was resolved quickly. It only took a couple of days for an update to filter through. The two clubs were talking.

'Liverpool and Sunderland are still working out the final details, but the deal is almost done,' his agent explained. 'You're going to be a Liverpool player before the weekend.'

Jordan felt the excitement rippling through him. He thought about him playing in that famous red shirt at Anfield, and sharing a dressing room with Stevie and Luis Suárez. Then his mind swung back to the sadness of leaving Sunderland, a club he had supported all his life.

The one thing he didn't think much about was the reaction to the transfer, and it caught him by surprise to see negative comments from a portion of the Liverpool fans. Maybe it was Jordan's limited Premier League experience, or maybe it was the disappointment that he wasn't an international star. But Jordan could feel the fans' frustration before he had even kicked a ball.

'I'll prove them all wrong,' he said, turning off the TV and going for a drive.

But he felt extra nervous as he arrived at Anfield for his introductory press conference. He knew the £16.75 million price tag attached to him would be mentioned and he just hoped there wouldn't be too many difficult questions.

'Wow, that's a bigger crowd of reporters than I'd expected,' he said a little shakily to one of the Liverpool media team.

'You'll get used to it,' the media rep replied. 'It's usually a packed room in here.'

Jordan felt the flash of cameras as he sat down next to Kenny Dalglish and Liverpool's other new signings, Stewart Downing and Charlie Adam.

'I'm over the moon, overjoyed to be here and I'm really looking forward to it,' he told reporters. 'Hopefully I can keep working hard, keep improving, and get my chance on the pitch.'

As Jordan walked out for his debut, the atmosphere at Anfield was electric. The crowd roared, before launching into their spine-tingling song, 'You'll Never

Walk Alone'. It gave Jordan goosebumps as he looked around at all the scarves being held up in the air.

But he was already seeing that the expectations at Liverpool were a level higher than at Sunderland. There was pressure to win every game, especially with this being described as a new era under Kenny.

Whether it was just a lack of understanding with his new teammates, or the nerves of his debut, Jordan felt tentative. His passing wasn't as crisp and a lot of his runs off the ball amounted to nothing. He was hardly surprised when he was subbed off in the second half.

Kenny shook Jordan's hand but could see the disappointment on his face. It wasn't the debut that Jordan had dreamed about, but now he just had to look ahead to the next game.

Another home game, this time against Bolton, provided a fresh chance to impress. As Luis lobbed a pass over the top for Stewart, Jordan raced forward to support the attack. Stewart's shot was well saved but it rebounded to Dirk Kuyt, who laid the ball back to Jordan. He instinctively took a first-time shot, which was blocked back into his path. But he didn't panic.

He just shifted the ball onto his left foot and, before any of the Bolton defenders could recover, he curled a shot into the top corner.

Goooooooooooooooooooaaaaaaaaaaaaaaaalllllllllllll llllllllllll!!!!!!!!!!!!!!!!!!!

His first Liverpool goal! He raced off to celebrate with the fans, hoping the goal would help to win them over. There was plenty of work ahead, but this certainly felt like a step in the right direction.

CHAPTER 15

WINNING THE
MIDFIELD BATTLE

'Have a seat, everyone,' Brendan Rodgers called out, signalling to the chairs which were arranged in neat rows. This was day one for Brendan after replacing Kenny as Liverpool manager.

Jordan picked up his bottle of water and sat down in the nearest chair, next to Stevie.

'We're setting out on an exciting journey here to get this club back to where it belongs,' Brendan said. 'At the top, winning trophies! I look forward to getting to know you all better during the weeks ahead.'

Brendan talked through his vision for how his Liverpool team would play. It centred around dominating possession with patient, short passing.

Jordan left the meeting with mixed feelings. He was ready for a better second season after a rocky start at Liverpool, but he was curious about whether he was going to be a good fit in Brendan's system. He was at his best when he used his energy to burst forward and play at pace. A slower build-up, on the other hand, favoured more technical players...

That nagging doubt only grew during the preseason, especially when Brendan brought in Joe Allen, a midfielder that he had worked with at Swansea in a similar system.

'How can I show what I can do if I'm glued to the bench?' Jordan said to Rebecca as she tried to take his mind off things with a trip to the cinema.

'Just stay ready,' Rebecca replied. 'You never know when your next chance will come.'

The signs were worrying, though. Ever since joining Liverpool, Jordan had tried to stay away from the TV and radio talk shows and the back pages of the newspapers. But he knew that some people were still saying things like 'a waste of money' and 'out of his depth'. That hurt.

But the latest rumours stung him even more. It sounded like Liverpool might be trying to sell him as part of a deal to sign midfielder Clint Dempsey from Fulham. Watching from the bench was hard enough, but would Liverpool really try to get rid of him so soon?

He just wanted to block out all of that noise. He went up to his bedroom, lay down on the bed and stared at the ceiling. How had this dream move gone so wrong? Tears streaked down his cheeks as he put his head in his hands.

Luckily, he had a great support system to lean on. Rebecca was full of encouragement, while his parents called most days to boost his spirits and his old coaches at Sunderland seemed to be taking turns to check in on him. The overall message was the same: keep your head down, be professional and your chance will come.

For now, Jordan was happy to trust in that. He had never backed away from a challenge and this was just another chance to show his resilience.

He was always among the first players to arrive, but now he made sure he got to the training ground fifteen minutes earlier. He also doubled the amount of time he spent in the weight room to put more muscle on his skinny frame.

Gradually, he adjusted to Brendan's style while still playing to his own strengths, and he made it clear that he was willing to fight for his place. By the start of the 2013–14 season, Jordan could see Brendan's opinion changing – a pat on the back here, words of praise there.

But off the field, he was about to enter an emotional time. One afternoon, Brian put a drink in front of Jordan and sat down opposite him at the kitchen table. 'Listen, son, there's something I need to tell you and I've been trying to find the right moment.'

Jordan sat completely still. This sounded serious.

'I've been at the hospital a lot this week,' Brian began. 'I've lost track of how many times, to be honest. They ran all kinds of tests and I got the results yesterday. I've got a serious illness and I'm going to need special care so I can start feeling better.'

Jordan felt his body go numb. His hand instinctively went to his mouth in shock.

'We're starting treatment and the doctors are confident they've caught it early,' Brian continued, with pain in his voice. 'But I don't want you to worry. I'm going to beat this. You just focus on your football. That will help me get through the next few months.'

Jordan couldn't find the right words, so he just got up and hugged his dad. 'You're a fighter,' he said quietly. 'If there's anything I can do to help, please tell me.'

He knew how much his dad loved going to watch him play – and how much it would hurt for him to have to watch on the TV instead for a while. But Jordan was determined to give him something to smile about.

Liverpool did just that with a thrilling title challenge. Luis and Daniel Sturridge were banging in the goals up front, Stevie was setting the tone in a deeper role and both Jordan and Philippe Coutinho had freedom to get forward.

Brendan brought Jordan into his office before training one morning with Liverpool placed top of the Premier League table. 'You and I got off to a bit

of a difficult start, but I'm so impressed with what
I've seen from you,' he said. 'You really look at home
in the system now and you've given us a big lift in
midfield with your energy.'

Jordan beamed. Walking away from Liverpool or
pushing for a transfer would have been the easy thing
to do, but that wasn't his style. Just like his dad, he
was a fighter.

Heading into the final month of the season, Jordan
felt great. Liverpool were still holding off Chelsea and
Manchester City, but the race was too close to call.

'We've got City next at Anfield, and that's a huge
one,' Jordan told Rebecca as they prepared the house
for the arrival of their first child that summer. 'We've
got to win that to keep our noses in front.'

It turned out to be a roller-coaster day. Liverpool
jumped into a 2–0 lead but were pegged back by two
City goals in the second half. With tension in the air, a
poor clearance trickled towards Philippe, who curled a
magical shot into the bottom corner.

Jordan jumped in the air and joined a group of red
shirts chasing Philippe over to the corner flag. That

had to be the winner!

But, with the adrenaline pumping, Jordan took a heavy touch and then clattered into Samir Nasri as he tried to win the ball back. He immediately knew he was in trouble, and he turned to see the referee showing him a red card.

Jordan walked off the pitch, still in shock. It was only when he was back in the dressing room that he thought about the suspension that would follow. 'I'm going to miss the next three games!' Jordan said to himself in the empty room, putting his head in his hands.

Without him, Liverpool faltered, with a 2–0 loss to Chelsea and a 3–3 draw with Crystal Palace. Meanwhile, City rallied to win the title by two points. There was nothing Brendan or Stevie could say to improve the mood in the dressing room on the final day of the season.

Jordan replayed his tackle against City countless times over the next week. Would things have been different if he had been available? He would never know. Jordan felt worst for Stevie. A Premier League winners medal would have been the perfect finale as his legendary Liverpool career edged towards the end.

It was a painful way to start the summer – and things got no better at the 2014 World Cup in Brazil. Jordan was delighted to be named in the England squad, but it was a short stay – they suffered losses to Italy and Uruguay to seal a group stage exit.

Playing in midfield next to Stevie and Wayne Rooney was something that Jordan would always remember, as was the pride of playing for his country at a World Cup – which he had thought about (and pretended to do) so many times as a young boy. He just wished that England had produced better results.

Still, Jordan was determined not to let these disappointments linger. He and Rebecca soon had baby Elexa to keep them busy – and he quickly saw that fatherhood would need his full attention.

CHAPTER 16

THE NEW STEVIE G?

'Shhhh!' whispered Dirk. 'He's coming.'

When Stevie walked into the cafeteria, Jordan and the rest of the squad popped out from around the corner, cheering and shouting.

It was Stevie's last training session as a Liverpool player after seventeen years as a professional at the club.

'Thanks, lads,' Stevie said, laughing as he wiped off some of the water that had been sprayed at him. 'It all still feels surreal. This club has been my life for so long.'

Jordan had learned so much from Stevie over the past few years and it was hard to imagine the dressing room, the flights, the training sessions and the matches without him.

As Jordan stretched, he could still feel the aches and pains of the last game. Luckily, he was due to get a massage that afternoon. Stevie sat down next to him. As usual, they were the first two players out there.

'Any chance I can talk you into staying for one more season?' Jordan said, grinning.

Stevie laughed. 'I'm getting that question a lot this week. But no, I've had an amazing career at Liverpool and this is the right time to walk away.'

'Well, at least promise you'll pay us a visit from time to time.'

'I will. But I know Liverpool are in good hands – and you're a big part of that, pal.'

Jordan looked up suddenly. 'Me?'

'Don't look so surprised! You're already the vice-captain. You've got the right attitude, the other lads respect you and you're getting better every year.'

'Well, I hope you know that a lot of that is because I've been able to learn so much from you,' Jordan replied, feeling a little emotional. 'I can't thank you enough for all the guidance you've given me, as a teammate and as a friend.'

As they bumped fists, Jordan was just sorry that they hadn't given Stevie a proper send-off by winning the league the prior season.

Before the summer break, Brendan called Jordan into his office. 'I think we've all earned a few months off,' he said. 'That was a draining season.'

Jordan nodded. 'Yeah, I'm looking forward to some time in the sun,' he replied. 'Then I'll be ready to roll again.'

'As you know, next year is the end of an era and the start of a new one,' Brendan added. 'I'll get right to the point – I want you to be the new Liverpool captain.'

Any thought that he would be able to play it cool went out of the window. Jordan felt his stomach drop and his legs shake. He smiled and then realised that Brendan was probably waiting for him to say something.

'Thanks for putting your faith in me,' Jordan managed, hearing his voice come out a little croakily. 'It'll be a dream come true to follow in the footsteps of so many great Liverpool captains.'

'You've earned it, Jordan,' Brendan continued. 'You stepped up when Stevie was out this season and the lads really responded to you. But no-one is expecting you to be Stevie. Be Jordan. We all know that you personify everything this club stands for.'

'Yeah, please don't let anyone label me as the new Stevie G!' Jordan said, laughing. 'Those are impossible boots to fill.'

'We've been thinking about the announcement, and we'll probably hold off until later in the summer. We don't want to do a press conference right after Stevie's last game, so just keep it to yourself until then.'

All the way home, Jordan wondered how many people he could tell without risking the story leaking out. In the end, he settled on just his parents and Jody, plus Rebecca, of course. It felt like the kind of news that he should share in person rather than over the phone, so he made dinner plans for that weekend.

Each time, he planned to wait until partway through the meal before his big announcement – and each time, he blurted it out before they even had drinks in their hands.

This was the start of a new chapter at Liverpool and Jordan had been trusted to lead the team forward.

CHAPTER 17

AN EXCITING
NEW ERA

As Jordan walked through the players' entrance at the Liverpool training ground, he could immediately feel that change was in the air. Jürgen Klopp had been appointed as the club's new manager during the international break and today was his first meeting with the first team squad.

Jordan knew all about Jürgen's success in Germany with Borussia Dortmund – two German league titles, one German cup and a trip to the 2013 Champions League Final. He had even watched a few clips of Jürgen's post-game interviews. While he might not have understood the words, the energy and passion of the manager jumped out of the screen.

The meeting room was quiet and tense. Jordan had seen enough managerial changes to know that this uneasiness was normal. He picked up a folder from the pile at the entrance and spotted Philippe, Adam Lallana and Daniel Sturridge sitting over on the left.

'So, what do you think?' Adam asked.

'Honestly, it's tough to see Brendan go, but I'm excited to see what's next,' Jordan replied. 'I think Jürgen can bring us back to the electric Anfield glory years.'

The room fell silent as Jürgen and a group of coaches walked into the room and stood at the front.

'Great to meet you all,' Jürgen said, smiling at everyone. 'Excuse the mistakes with my English, but I'm trying!'

'It's already better than our German, boss,' Jordan called out, making everyone laugh.

'Liverpool is a great club with a great history,' Jürgen continued. 'Together, we're going to add to that history. The biggest thing I ask from you is to give me everything. We're going to push you hard, but we'll do it with a smile.'

Jordan nodded and saw other teammates doing the same. Jürgen certainly had grabbed their attention.

'If you've read anything about me, you'll know the German word Gegenpressing,' Jürgen continued. 'That's the approach I want to bring here. We press high. We press quick. We press together. Then if we get that right, it's a beautiful thing. True heavy metal football.'

Jürgen answered questions, introduced his coaches and laid out the plan for the rest of the week. After the players headed off to the dressing room to get ready for training, Jordan could hear the buzz down the corridor. There was a belief rippling through the squad. Clearly, Jürgen saw a path for Liverpool to be competing for major trophies again.

Even so, Jürgen's style would come at a price, with more running and intensity for everyone, from the strikers to the defenders. Jordan was still dealing with foot and heel injuries, but he was happy to be at the sessions on the touchline. From midfield, he could see what his role would be in sparking the press and he even caught himself yelling out instructions in the training drills.

'Your man, Philippe!'

'Squeeze up and cut that off, Adam!'

The fans were dreaming of trophies again too. 'You should hear the radio phone-in shows,' Brian explained on the phone one evening. 'A few weeks ago, every question was about what the players were doing wrong. Now it's about transfer targets and your chances of the top four!'

In a way, Jordan's injuries meant that he got to spend extra time with Jürgen and the coaches in the first few months. That gave him an even clearer understanding of the new playing style and an up-close look at the restless energy that Jürgen brought every day.

While Jordan warmed up in front of a packed Anfield crowd for his first game back, he felt a few nerves. He wanted to impress Jürgen and show that he knew the pressing game plan inside-out.

Within the first few minutes, Jordan got the fans on their feet with a crunching tackle and a trademark interception. Later in the half, he saw the ball laid off to Philippe and pushed forward. As soon as Philippe glided a cross into the box, Jordan gambled with a run in behind his marker.

Adam headed the ball down and it landed perfectly for Jordan to sweep a quick shot into the net.

Goooooooooooooooooooooaaaaaaaaaaaaaaaaaallllllllllllll llllllllllllll!!!!!!!!!!!!!!!!!!!!!!

Jordan raced off to celebrate, blowing a kiss before he was wrapped in hugs. Over on the touchline, Jürgen was punching the air in celebration. Jordan looked over and felt ten feet tall when he saw Jürgen giving him a thumbs up.

Though the final score, a 2–2 draw, wasn't the result that Jordan was hoping for, he could see the Liverpool reset taking shape.

A Europa League tie against Manchester United was another chance for Liverpool to show off their new identity. 'Anfield is going to be rocking tonight,' Jordan said as he and Adam arrived at the stadium four hours before kick-off.

'We've got to feed off the fans,' Adam added. 'Let's show them this isn't the same Liverpool that they've been pushing around for the last ten years.'

Jürgen was bouncing around with more energy than ever. 'Don't let them settle,' he instructed, with a whirlwind of gestures. 'High energy from the first minute.'

Jordan set the tone as Liverpool made a flying start and took control of the midfield. Daniel opened the scoring with a penalty, Roberto Firmino added a second and Jordan went close with a first-time shot that flew just wide. Jürgen looked like he was kicking and heading every ball from the touchline.

'That could have been 5–0!' Jordan said, with a big grin, as he and Adam walked off at full-time.

Though injuries limited him over the rest of the season, Jordan's excitement about the club's future outweighed the frustration of regular trips for treatment. Maybe Liverpool weren't title contenders yet, but he felt sure that Jürgen had put them on the path to major trophies.

CHAPTER 18

ON THE TREATMENT TABLE AGAIN

'So, is this the year that Liverpool bring the league title home?' Brian asked. He and Jordan were tucking into lunch in the back garden surrounded by glorious sunshine, while toasting his continued recovery from his illness.

'We've made some big strides under Jürgen,' Jordan replied. 'On our day, we can take any team apart, but the next test is finding the consistency to grind out wins the way that City and Chelsea can. With Jürgen, one thing you know for sure is that we'll give it our best shot.'

Brian grinned. It was easy to imagine Jürgen plotting Liverpool's title challenge all summer. He had already made one key move, snapping up attacker Sadio Mané from Southampton.

'To be honest, my number-one goal for this year is to stay fit,' Jordan explained, as he checked the pram where little Alba, his youngest daughter, was sleeping. 'I missed too many games last season going in and out of the treatment room. My form really suffered.'

'How do you feel so far?' Brian replied. He'd had an up-close view of Jordan's injury struggles and knew it would probably take a few months for his son to really trust his heel and knee again.

'Great.... touch wood,' Jordan said, tapping the wooden placemat. 'But ask me again when we're playing three games a week!'

The biggest development during the preseason was a new role for Jordan. In one of the earliest training sessions, Jürgen approached him during a break.

'We're going to try some different things over the next few weeks and one of them is putting you in more of a holding role in front of the defence. It'll allow you to get on the ball more, but will mean a different mindset from a box-to-box role.'

By this point, Jordan had complete trust in Jürgen. While he had always loved getting forward into positions to shoot or to set up his teammates, he was willing to take on whatever role helped the team. 'Sure, let's try it. I like the idea of being able to influence the game more in a deeper position.'

There were some rocky moments at first. Jordan had to retrain his brain on how to react to certain situations. He would find himself sprinting forward, then realising that was out of position if Liverpool lost the ball. But Jürgen had seen enough to know that there was potential.

When the Liverpool players arrived at Stamford Bridge for a September clash with Chelsea, there was a more serious mood on the team bus. Jordan couldn't quite explain it – there were still lots of laughs, but they all had a more focused look in their eyes as they headed for the dressing rooms.

Jordan saw the captain's armband laid out at his locker next to his 'Henderson 14' shirt. Today, in particular, he was determined to set an example.

Defender Dejan Lovren scored a rare goal from

Philippe's perfect cross to give Liverpool the lead and
Jordan was winning the battle against N'Golo Kanté
and Nemanja Matić in midfield. With the Chelsea
fans getting restless, Jordan buzzed around to tighten
the press.

Adam tried to skip inside from the left wing but the
ball was cleared as far as Jordan. He was twenty-five
yards out, but he took one touch to cushion it before
whipping an unstoppable, dipping strike into the top
corner. *2–0!*

Goooooooooooooooooooaaaaaaaaaaaaaaaalllllllllllllllllllllllllll!!!!!!!!!!!!!!!!!!!!!!!

He was jogging away as soon as he hit it, arm in the
air, acting as if this was something he did every day.
Dejan and Adam were the first to catch up with him.
'Worldie!' Adam screamed, jumping on Jordan's back.
'What a goal!'

Chelsea pulled a goal back, but Liverpool survived
for a statement win. Jürgen was on the pitch,
congratulating his players and saving his biggest
hug for Jordan. While they celebrated with the fans
at the far end of the stadium, Jordan could feel the

confidence building.

Heading into 2017, Jordan knew that a top four finish (and qualification for the Champions League) was within Liverpool's grasp. 'We can't let things slip now,' he told his teammates during one January training session. 'Let's keep pushing each other to get better.' Their chances seemed even stronger after signing Virgil van Dijk from Southampton.

But Jordan's season came to an end with one accidental collision in training. Reaching to control a loose ball, he felt a kick on his foot as a teammate tried to get there first. Jordan yelped and ended up on the ground. The pain was bad enough that he had to limp back to the main building for more tests.

Initially, there was good news. 'No sign of a fracture,' the club doctor explained later that week. 'But I can see the bruising is even worse today than it was when we did the X-ray. Can you put any weight on it?'

Jordan shook his head. 'Not really,' he said. He got up to demonstrate and had to clutch the side of the treatment table to keep his balance.

His recovery took longer than expected, and he was

stuck in another frustrating spell of rest and treatment. As his teammates battled for points, he was limited to a cheerleader role. He did his best to stay positive and share any ideas that might help the team, but he had never been good at watching from the bench.

Eventually, the only real choice was for Jordan to be shut down until next season. Of course, he hated that idea, but he understood the risk of re-injuring his foot. 'That's two years in a row now where injuries have ruined things,' he told Rebecca after getting the latest update. 'It's just cruel not to be able to do what I love.'

But Rebecca and the girls could make any situation better. 'Don't worry, Daddy,' Elexa told him that night. 'You'll be even better once the doctors have mended you.'

She gave him a kiss and a big hug. While that couldn't heal his foot, it was the next best thing.

CHAPTER 19

CHAMPIONS LEAGUE DESPAIR

'These big European nights at Anfield are electric,' Jordan told Rebecca one afternoon, as he got ready to leave for the latest Champions League game. 'It's the same number of fans in the same stadium... but it's an even more amazing atmosphere.'

With Jordan fully fit again, Liverpool were continuing their momentum – and they saved their most magical performances for the Champions League, with new signing Mo Salah in unstoppable form. With a sky-high feeling of belief, they swept past each hurdle in Europe, knocking out Porto, Manchester City and Roma to set up a Champions League final against Real Madrid.

The celebrations in the dressing room after a nervy finish to the semi-final second leg against Roma were a mixture of joy and relief. Liverpool had won the first leg 5–2 at Anfield but had to sweat out a 4–2 loss in Rome. 'Never in doubt!' Jürgen joked, with his face confirming the stress of that second half.

Jordan, Trent and Virgil snapped photos as the achievement of reaching the final sunk in. But they all knew that the job wasn't done yet. The toughest part was still to come.

When the Liverpool players arrived in Kiev for the final, Jordan tried to savour the moment. 'Put aside the pressure of the final for a few minutes,' his dad had urged him. 'Remember the nine-year-old Jordan and what this kind of moment would have meant to him. You just never know when this opportunity will come up again.'

On the day of the game, before getting into his warm-up kit, Jordan joined Mo and Virgil on the Kiev pitch. At first, they chatted about the flight, the hotel and their path through the competition. Then they all went silent. Jordan was busy visualising the game that lay ahead: how he'd cover every blade of grass to slow down a slick Real Madrid midfield.

When he led the Liverpool players out of the dressing room and into the tunnel, Jordan was surrounded by all the usual Champions League logos and signs. But this felt different. Even the Champions League anthem seemed more spine-tingling. Maybe that had something to do with the Champions League trophy that was perched on a stand pitchside, with red and white ribbons on the handles. If everything went to plan, Jordan would be lifting that trophy in two hours' time.

But there was a game to win first. When the referee blew his whistle for the coin toss, Jordan jogged over and shook hands with Sergio Ramos, the Real captain. By now, the fans were making themselves heard, with 'You'll Never Walk Alone' belting out from the Liverpool sections of the stadium. Stretching his calves and hamstrings one final time, Jordan could feel his heart beating faster.

He settled these nerves with some early touches, and he, James and Gini Wijnaldum were quickly scurrying from side to side to win back possession.

Mo and Sadio had shots blocked, then Trent's low strike was well saved. 'Lovely football, lads!' Jordan called, clapping loudly. 'Keep it going.'

Before half-time, the ball bounced forward towards Mo, who darted in front of Ramos. They both fell to the ground, with their arms tangled. Ramos popped back up, but Mo stayed down. Jordan's stomach dropped as he jogged over.

Holding his shoulder, Mo had tears in his eyes as the Liverpool physio helped him off the field, and Jordan knew that was the end of Mo's night.

Now Jordan realised his leadership was more important than ever, and he tried to rally his teammates. They needed to believe that Liverpool could still win without their star man.

As Jordan led his teammates back out for the second half, he knew that the next fifteen minutes would be crucial. Real were sure to come flying out of the blocks, and part of Jordan's job was to track back and help Trent against Ronaldo.

One long pass skipped through to Liverpool

goalkeeper Loris Karius, and Jordan turned to jog
up the field. Then he heard a roar from the crowd
and turned back to see the ball trickling into the
Liverpool net.

'What... what happened?' he shouted, looking for
answers from his defenders and the referee, who was
signalling for a goal.

Loris was pleading with the assistant referee. Virgil
and Trent had their hands on their heads.

'Loris went to throw it out quickly and it rebounded
in off Benzema's leg,' Trent explained, with shock all
over his face.

The anger and frustration would have to wait,
though. The goal was given and now Liverpool had to
find a way back into the game. Jordan signalled for his
teammates to switch on again. There was still plenty
of time to fight back.

Liverpool won a corner on the right and Jordan
gestured for Virgil and Dejan to get into the box.
He dropped back to cover for them.

Trent swung in the corner and Dejan won the
header in front of Ramos. The ball looped towards

the goal, then Sadio stuck out his foot, directing a shot into the net. Jordan leapt in the air. 1–1. Game on.

But less than ten minutes later, out of nowhere, Liverpool had a mountain to climb again as Gareth Bale's acrobatic bicycle kick flew into the top corner. Jordan stood open-mouthed. He could probably play in another hundred finals and not see a more spectacular goal than that!

As Liverpool charged forward in search of another goal, disaster struck again. Bale struck a swerving long shot straight at Loris, who misjudged it and ended up just palming it into the net.

At the final whistle, the emotions poured out. While the Real players celebrated at one end of the stadium, the tears flowed for Jordan, and Jürgen wrapped him in a hug.

Jordan felt worst for Loris, whose two mistakes would be played over and over again for the next few weeks. He found his goalkeeper and tried his best to console him. 'Listen, pal, we win together and we lose together,' he said, gently. 'Remember that. We're a team and we're here for you.'

The Liverpool dressing room was silent as the players showered and changed – so silent that they could hear the Real celebrations from the other dressing room. Eventually, Jordan stood up and walked into the middle of the room.

'Tonight is going to sting for a while, lads, but we'll be back. Let's make that promise to each other right now. We'll be back in another Champions League final together and we'll finish the job.'

One by one, his teammates nodded.

Jürgen walked over to join Jordan. 'Hendo's right,' he said, putting his hand on his captain's shoulder. 'Be proud of what you've all achieved this year and let this pain fuel you for next season. We'll be even stronger after this experience.'

CHAPTER 20

WORLD CUP 2018: ENGLAND ON THE RISE IN RUSSIA

'I've played in lots of big games but this one feels on a whole different level,' Jordan explained to Liz as they spoke on the phone before England's last 16 knockout round match against Colombia at the 2018 World Cup. 'I think we're starting to move on from some of our nightmare exits from previous tournaments.'

Jordan had watched from the bench in horror when England crashed out of Euro 2016 against Iceland. But there was a different vibe around the camp now, as Gareth Southgate continued to put his stamp on the team.

Here at the World Cup in Russia, England had qualified from their group in second place and suddenly their side of the draw had opened up invitingly.

'If we get through this one, we'll be favourites in the next...' Liz began.

'Mum!' Jordan interrupted. 'What have you always told me about taking it one game at a time?!'

Liz laughed. 'Just testing you to make sure you weren't looking too far ahead. The whole country is behind you. You should see all the flags and banners on our street.'

Jordan went through a longer warm-up than usual and chatted with Eric Dier and Kieran Trippier. He knew he had pushed his body hard and the last thing he wanted was to limp off with a pulled muscle.

'It's going to be another hot one today,' Gareth reminded the players.

'No kidding, boss,' said Raheem, taking a towel and wiping the sweat from his forehead.

'Keep the ball and be patient. Let Colombia do the chasing. Most of all, don't fall into any of their little traps. Stay cool and calm.'

The national anthem blared around the stadium. Jordan felt the hairs standing on end on his arms and his neck. He had been a regular in England squads over the past few years, but there was still nothing quite like putting on the England shirt and playing for his country.

Colombia played exactly as Gareth and the coaches had discussed all week. They were physical in midfield, with ten men behind the ball to frustrate the England attack. When the ball went up to Harry Kane, the defenders were quick to swarm around him, snapping at his ankles.

Harry won a free kick just before half-time and Kieran prepared to whip a shot towards the Colombia goal. As planned, Jordan got into position on the end of the Colombia wall, trying to block the keeper's view.

But a Colombia defender was pushing Jordan out of the way. Jordan stood his ground and then felt the defender throw a headbutt at his jaw. He fell backwards as Harry rushed over to the referee. But there was no red card. It was the type of moment that Gareth had warned the team about and Jordan was quickly back in peacemaker mode, trying to make sure none of his teammates overreacted.

With his jaw still aching, Jordan drove England forward in the second half. They won a corner – and then a penalty when Harry was thrown to the floor. As Jordan watched nervously at the edge of the box, Harry calmly slotted the penalty down the middle past the diving goalkeeper. *1–0!*

That settled the nerves. Gareth made a couple of defensive changes but a late Colombia rally pushed England onto the back foot. Pickford flew to his left to tip a shot over the bar, then came the last-gasp drama. A corner from the right dropped invitingly in the penalty area and a Colombia defender headed the ball powerfully towards goal. It bounced up and into the roof of the net. *1–1!*

Jordan looked to the sky and took a deep breath. Time to start all over again.

'Put that behind you,' urged Gareth. 'We've been the better team. Let's look for a winner in extra-time.' Jordan guzzled water and stretched his legs.

Thirty minutes later, it was still 1–1 and the game would be decided via the dreaded penalty shootout. Penalties had been a key topic with Gareth since the very first training session at the tournament. Jordan knew that this England team was better prepared for a shootout than any other squad he had been part of.

He had been hitting his penalties sweetly in training and he didn't hesitate to raise his hand. Gareth put him on the third spot-kick. Jordan joined his teammates in giving Pickford a good-luck fist bump then linking arms on the halfway line. He could barely watch.

The first five penalties all flew into the net. When England were trailing 3–2, Jordan started the long walk to the penalty spot. Pickford appeared holding the ball. 'Good luck, pal,' he said, handing the ball to Jordan.

Jordan placed it carefully on the spot and then took five steps backwards for his run-up. The whistle blew and he struck his penalty hard and low, but the Colombia goalkeeper had guessed correctly and made a one-handed save.

The disappointment spread across Jordan's face. It was a decent penalty but when he watched it again, he questioned if he had made it too obvious that he was aiming for that corner.

Now all he could do was hope. Harry stepped forward to put an arm round him. 'Unlucky, Hendo,' he said. 'You hit that well.'

The next Colombia penalty rebounded off the bar and England were back in business. Jordan felt the panic ease. Kieran calmly pinged his penalty into the top corner and it was all square again.

By now, Jordan couldn't stand still. He was swaying, bouncing… and then jumping as Pickford sprung to his right to save the next penalty. Eric had the chance to end it and Jordan gave him a pat on the back as he stepped forward.

The next ten seconds felt like ten minutes. Eric placed the ball on the spot and eyed up the net. The referee blew his whistle and Eric fired a low penalty to the keeper's right. When the ball rolled into the bottom corner, Jordan leapt in the air and joined the group racing over to celebrate. England's penalty jinx was over!

'I guess I really owe you one now,' he said, high-fiving Pickford as the players jogged over to the largest section of England fans in the crowd.

A routine 2–0 win over Sweden in the quarter-finals put England through to the World Cup semi-finals for the first time since 1990. 'We're ninety minutes away from the World Cup final,' he repeated again and again to his parents that week. 'It's still sinking in.'

Jordan knew that their toughest task lay ahead now – beating Croatia. He knew all about their quality after chasing Luka Modrić around the pitch in the Champions League Final, and Gareth was quick to highlight that as Jordan's main assignment for the semi-final. 'Everything flows through Modrić,' Gareth explained. 'If we can crowd him and force him deep to get on the ball, it'll take a lot of the sting out of their attacks.'

As if that challenge wasn't daunting enough, Jordan was also battling injury. There was nothing that could stop him playing in a World Cup semi-final, but his hamstring made him wince whenever he had to change direction. With the anthem and the noise from the England fans making him forget all about the pain, Jordan settled in for one of the biggest games of his career.

Dele Alli made an early run and was tripped on the edge of the box. As Kieran lined up the free kick, Jordan took up his usual spot on the end of the wall, trying to alter the Croatia wall and block the goalkeeper's view. Kieran stepped up and fizzed a free kick right over Jordan's head and into the top corner. England were off to a dream start.

But the second half was a different story. Croatia pulled level and dominated possession in midfield. Though Jordan kept running, he could feel the game slipping away. Sensing that he had given everything he had, Gareth subbed him off in extra-time. Jordan then watched in agony as Croatia struck again with a late winner.

Noooooooooooo! Jordan felt numb as he trudged onto the pitch to shake hands and console his teammates. In a daze, he walked over to applaud the England fans. It had been a great run and he knew that he would eventually look back on this tournament with huge pride. But for now, in this moment, it stung as badly as any defeat in his life.

'You've given the whole country an incredible

summer, son,' Brian said as they digested the result together that night. Jordan was having no luck falling asleep.

'I know one thing for certain heading into next season,' Jordan answered. 'I'm sick of coming up short in these big tournaments and watching others celebrating with the trophies. The next chance we get, I'm not letting it slip through my fingers.'

CHAPTER 21

CHAMPIONS LEAGUE DELIGHT

'It's not over,' Jordan said, sounding calmer than he was expected to be. 'We had a bad game and now we've got to dig ourselves out of this hole.'

Brian nodded because it seemed like the right thing to do. Maybe Jordan just needed someone else to agree with him. But most of his friends who had watched Liverpool's 3–0 loss to Barcelona in the first leg of the Champions League semi-final seemed to have a different opinion. It had been a disaster.

But while the Liverpool players prepared for the second leg, Jürgen had the same positive thoughts as Jordan. 'You know the Barcelona players will feel they've done their job already in this semi-final,' he said. 'They'll be thinking about the final, the trophy, the parade. If we can just crack open the door slightly, I know we can smash through it.'

'Let's launch into the first ten minutes,' Jordan added. 'If we get an early goal, you know the atmosphere is going to be electric. I don't care how many trophies those guys have won, a rocking Anfield does crazy things to teams.'

The task would be tougher with Mo out injured, but Jordan still believed it could be a famous night. Divock Origi would be starting up front and Jordan made sure he was paired up with him during the warm-up.

'This is your moment, big fella,' Jordan said, putting an arm round Divock. 'You've got the pace and strength to scare them. Get yourself in the box and we'll find you.'

Sure enough, Anfield was already buzzing, seemingly unaware of the damaging first-leg loss. As 'You'll Never Walk Alone' swept around the stadium, Jordan felt the usual Champions League goosebumps mixed with fierce determination. All season, he had wanted to get back to the Champions League Final and make amends for last year. There was still a chance that he would.

Playing next to Fabinho and James, Jordan had clear instructions to push forward and link with the front three. He did just that early on. First, he almost got on the end of a low cross to the back post inside the first minute, before a long ball found Sadio, who cushioned a layoff into Jordan's path. The ball got stuck under his feet but he still managed to poke a low left-footed shot towards the bottom corner. The Barcelona keeper got a hand to it, but Divock was in the perfect place for a tap-in. 1–0, and just seven minutes gone!

Anfield erupted as Jordan raced over to celebrate. 'Let's go!' he screamed to the fans.

Liverpool rode their luck and needed a few good stops from Allison. Jordan had a snapshot blocked as they counter-attacked at a frantic pace. A 1–0 half-time scoreline was solid, but there was a lot more work to be done.

Gini came on for the second half, with James dropping to left back. Now both Jordan and Gini would be joining the attack. Trent burst free on the right and swept in a cross. Gini met it with a first time shot that crashed into the net. *2–0!*

Two minutes later, Gini did it again. The cross came from the left this time and Gini rose to place a header into the corner. *3–0!*

The noise was deafening. Jordan and Trent raced over to celebrate in the corner. They had achieved an unthinkable fightback. 'Now let's go and win this!' Jordan yelled, high-fiving all his teammates. 'They're rattled. Keep attacking.'

With just over ten minutes to go, Liverpool won a corner on the right. Trent jogged over to take it but was about to leave the ball for an in-swinger instead. Then he glanced up and saw Barcelona totally unprepared for the corner, with Divock standing alone in the six-yard box. Trent whipped it in quickly and Divock didn't even need to move. He just swung his right foot and swept the ball into the corner. *4–0!*

Now they just had to hold on. Jordan didn't stop running, intercepting passes and thumping the ball as far down the pitch as possible. When the referee blew the final whistle, there were bodies on the ground everywhere – Barcelona players in shock covering their faces and Liverpool players overwhelmed by the miraculous performance. Mo strolled onto the pitch with a huge smile wearing a 'Never Give Up' T-shirt.

As Jordan floated over to applaud the Liverpool crowd, it didn't seem like a single fan had left early. The party was just starting.

'I love you guys and I believe in you, but I still don't know how you did it!' Jürgen said, grinning, as the players finally took a minute to sit down and digest the night.

Jordan could hardly move. He was exhausted physically and mentally. But he couldn't remember feeling happier about any win in his whole life. What a game!

'I told you it wasn't over!' he joked, hugging his parents.

'I think that's the most incredible game of football I've ever seen,' Brian said, with tears in his eyes. 'And you were phenomenal.'

Jordan allowed himself to ride the wave of joy for a

couple more days, but then he was back in big-game mode. Liverpool would have to beat Tottenham in Madrid to banish the ghosts of last season and add to the club's long European history.

The good news was that Mo would be back. After his agony in the 2018 final, he deserved a second chance more than anyone. 'Well, let's just see if you can get back in the team now,' Jordan joked, as Mo pretended to punch him on the arm.

Arriving in Madrid, Jordan had flashbacks to the 2018 final. But he knew that the squad had learned a lot from that night.

'After last season, we owe it to ourselves to finish the job,' he said, as he walked into the hotel meeting room with Sadio and Allison.

'The next time we're on the team plane, it's going to be as Champions League winners,' Sadio said. 'That's what we have to believe.'

It was strange to be facing another Premier League team in a big European final. He knew what to expect from Tottenham, with Harry Kane and Son Heung-min as the big threats. But equally it would be hard to spring many surprises on them after playing each other already that year.

As the Champions League anthem belted out again, Jordan knew how fortunate he was. Most players didn't get to experience one final on this stage. He was about to play in his second straight Champions League final.

All week, Jürgen had talked about making a fast start, knowing that Tottenham would likely be the more nervous team. Jordan reminded his teammates as they waited for kick-off. 'Let's get after them in the first ten minutes, lads. No time on the ball, no easy passes. Make them feel a sea of red shirts.'

A good interception and long pass sent Sadio free on the left. He cut inside and clipped the ball into the penalty area. It rebounded off a Tottenham player's arm. 'Handball!' Jordan screamed. Yes, he was a long way back down the pitch, but it looked close.

The referee pointed to the spot, and Mo grabbed the ball. He drilled home the penalty as the Liverpool fans roared. Jordan was one of the first players to reach Mo to celebrate, waving to urge the fans to get even louder.

It was the dream start. With Tottenham rattled, Jordan flew around midfield to win every tackle. The through-ball to Mo and Sadio always seemed to be an option and then it was up to Jordan and James to get into the box with Roberto.

But at 1–0, nothing was safe. Tottenham started to create chances in the second half and Jordan was spending more and more time tracking back. Jürgen was up on the touchline, signalling for more energy.

'Keep them calm!' he called to Jordan during a break in play. 'Pull Roberto a little deeper to help.'

There were nervy moments – desperate headers, sliding blocks and hurried clearances. But then Divock came off the bench and calmed everyone down. A Liverpool corner bounced around on the edge of the box before landing at Divock's left foot. He fired home an unstoppable skidding shot.

Jordan could breathe again. With his arms outstretched, he ran over to join the pile of red shirts in front of the Liverpool fans. There were wild scenes in the crowd, with fans falling over each other in the joy of the moment.

'We've done it, lads,' Jordan yelled, hugging Divock and Virgil. 'That trophy is ours!'

When the whistle blew, Jordan raised his arms in the air, then his hands over his head. It was the moment that he had dreamed about for so many months, finally banishing the nightmares from last year's final. He found Virgil, Mo, Trent and so many other players who had been through the battles with him over the last year. Then Jürgen appeared, wrapping Jordan in one of his bear hugs.

A year ago, Jordan had walked straight past the trophy without even glancing at it. It was too painful. Now, he couldn't wait to see it. He watched from the back of the line as the medals were handed out, then made his way forward, with all the emotion of the journey bubbling up.

He lowered his head to receive his medal and then carried the trophy over to where his teammates were already starting the party. As the fireworks went off around them, Jordan lifted the trophy high above his head.

'Yeaaaaaah!' he screamed.

There was still time for a victory lap, with thousands of Liverpool fans staying for a glimpse of their heroes with the trophy. As they made it to the far corner of the stadium, Jordan spotted his dad down near the front row.

Brian managed to talk his way on to the pitch and soon he and Jordan were standing together in a tearful hug. It all spilled out for Jordan in that moment – his dad's support throughout his career, the battle with his illness and the pride of winning this trophy in front of him.

'You've done it!' Brian said, as Jordan got ready to rejoin his teammates. 'I knew you would.'

CHAPTER 22

HAPPY FAMILIES

There was a knock on the living room door and Elexa and Alba walked in.

'Daddy, you're invited to my special football tea party,' Elexa said.

Jordan looked up and smiled. 'Wow, that sounds lovely.'

No matter how tense and tiring things got with Liverpool and England, it usually only took a few minutes at home with Rebecca and the kids to clear Jordan's mind.

'It's starting in five minutes – and it's very impolite to be late,' Elexa added.

'Well, we can't have that then,' Jordan said,

laughing. 'I'll come up with you now.'

Elexa smiled at her little sister and they both rushed off upstairs. Jordan followed them.

Sure enough, the playroom was set up for a tea party, with a toy teapot, little cups and saucers. Rebecca was already sitting at the little table and there was an extra chair, with 'Daddy' written on a slip of paper just in front of it.

'How have I never been to this place before?' he asked. 'It looks perfect.'

'The food will be ready soon,' Alba said. 'We've got cucumber sandwiches and... erm...'

She rushed over to Rebecca. 'What was the other thing called, Mummy?'

'Scones,' Rebecca replied, smiling.

'Oh yes, scones with jam and cream.'

'Wow,' Jordan said. 'I can't wait to try those. I'm really hungry.'

Jordan saw that they had set up their little football net in the far corner.

'That's for after the food,' Elexa said, seeing Jordan looking across the room. 'We can all play together.'

'Well, only if Daddy has eaten all of his sandwiches, right?' Rebecca added, struggling not to laugh.

These were the priceless moments that Jordan was so desperate not to miss out on, despite all of his commitments at Liverpool and the midweek travel for Champions League games.

As he grinned at Elexa and pretended to tuck into plastic sandwiches, there was nowhere that Jordan would have rather been. He didn't even put up any resistance when Elexa appeared with her tiaras and started handing them out.

After the 'meal', the girls cleared away the plates and returned with scones – which looked a lot like building blocks from the toy chest. 'Delicious!' he said, winking at Alba.

Then it was time for the football party of the event. The girls changed out of their dresses and into their 'Henderson 14' shirts. Jordan laughed as they both did their best impressions of him with a mini football.

'Daddy, when can we come to see one of your games again?' Elexa asked. 'We want to see you win one of those big cups.'

'Well, that doesn't happen all the time, sadly,' Jordan said, smiling. 'But we can plan something soon for you girls to come to Anfield. You're usually a good luck charm for me when you're in the crowd.'

'But it's very loud,' Alba added. 'Last time, Mummy had to put her hands over my ears a few times.'

'That might also have been so that you didn't hear what the fans were saying to the referee!' Rebecca chimed in, laughing.

The tea party stretched on late into the afternoon, and Jordan was reminded once again of how lucky he was. Family life brought him so many happy moments and the kind of balance that made him a better footballer and captain too.

'Anyone still hungry after that feast?' he asked, smiling. The girls' hands went straight up. 'Right then, the only way to follow up a football tea party is with pizza night, I think.'

Elexa and Alba cheered. 'Thank you!' they shouted, rushing over and jumping on Jordan, who was soon at the bottom of the pile but perfectly happy to be there.

CHAPTER 23

A HERO ON AND OFF THE PITCH

The dramatic, unforgettable European nights from the last two seasons had put Liverpool on the map again. But Jordan knew that the next step was bringing the Premier League trophy back to Anfield.

'This is going to be our year,' Jordan said, jogging around the training pitch next to Trent and Andy Robertson. 'I can feel it.'

'We've got all the pieces now,' Trent replied. 'Everyone is talking about City, but we can match them.'

Jürgen made it clear during the preseason that he wanted Liverpool to be in the hunt for all the trophies this year. 'Let's be greedy!' he said, with his usual huge grin.

But he reminded the squad that it was almost thirty years since the club had won the league title. Jordan recalled that comment just floating in the air for a few minutes, as all the players absorbed it.

Liverpool had come close the previous year, finishing as runners-up, just one point behind Manchester City in an intense topsy-turvy two-horse title race. The hunger was clear in the way that Liverpool began the 2019–20 Premier League season, but a visit from an experienced City team in November would be the ultimate measuring stick. Jordan could hardly sleep that week as the game plan whirled around in his head. A win would take Liverpool nine points clear at the top of the table.

'Let's make a statement today,' Jürgen said, as the players slotted in their shin pads and taped their ankles. 'We're coming for the trophy!'

Jordan led the way down the tunnel and Anfield erupted. It felt as loud as a European night, with all the fans knowing how big this game was.

The drama started early. City screamed for a penalty

when the ball bounced up towards Trent's hand in the box, before Liverpool counter-attacked with Sadio. A half clearance reached Fabinho and he rocketed a shot into the City net. While Jordan tried to get in the middle of the scrum of City players surrounding the referee, they were all waiting to see if the goal would stand. After a lengthy review, it did – *1–0 to Liverpool!*

With temperatures rising on both teams, Liverpool swept forward again. Trent to Andy to Mo. *BANG – 2–0!* Anfield was rocking.

But City kept coming as the game swung from end to end. Jordan tried to stay calm and shield the defence as much as possible. But that was no easy task against Kevin De Bruyne and Sergio Agüero.

In the second half, Jordan received a pass on the right and looked up. With no-one in the box, he rolled back the clock to his days on the right wing for Sunderland, dribbling forward and pushing the ball ahead to create space for a cross.

With little space to work with, Jordan still managed to wrap his foot round the ball and curl a deep cross towards the back post. Sadio arrived right on time to head the ball home. 3–0!

Sadio ran to the fans. Trent and Fabinho ran to Jordan. They all ended up on the far side as a frenzy swept around Anfield.

City pulled a goal back and still forced a few nervy moments, but soon the Liverpool party could start.

'We played like champions today!' Jordan said to Trent and Sadio, while they all applauded the fans. 'Now we've just got to keep it going.'

Over the next few months, Liverpool were relentless. The front three of Mo, Sadio and Roberto were tearing defences apart, with Jordan helping to pull the strings in midfield.

As it turned out, the only thing that could slow them down was COVID-19. In March 2020, it was announced that the Premier League season would have to be suspended, but for how long was still uncertain. No-one knew quite how to handle the unexpected break, but Jordan tried to stick to his usual routine as much as possible, eating the right food and exercising at home.

Jürgen and his coaches began preparing video sessions for everything from gym work to nutrition. For Jordan, it was nice to have extra time at home with Rebecca and the kids, but he was soon looking for ways to step up to help others who were struggling.

He started discussions with the LFC Foundation for a donation to support the North Liverpool Foodbank, then launched into plans to help charities tied to the national healthcare system. His efforts even got recognition from the Queen.

'We've got to do more, lads,' he pleaded on a call with captains from the other Premier League clubs. 'If we build the Players Together fund, we can make a real difference at a time when so many people need support.'

Jürgen and the rest of the squad were fully behind him, as Jordan continued to call for more funding. 'I love it,' Jürgen said, laughing in admiration at Jordan's relentless fundraising. 'You've created a pressing system off the field too!'

When the season finally restarted in June 2020, Jordan knew that his main job was to make sure that the team had the right level of focus, especially as there would be strict rules about fans in the stadiums. Yes, Liverpool's lead had ballooned at the top but he refused to have any talk of the Premier League title until the trophy was mathematically theirs.

Finally, that day arrived. The party could start. As Jordan walked the steps of The Kop to collect his Premier League winners medal and lift the trophy, his only regret was that Anfield was empty. He hoped the Liverpool fans across the country and around the world were finding their own ways to celebrate.

Jürgen shook Jordan's hand as they made their way back inside. 'What a season!' he said. 'You're the heartbeat of this team, Hendo, and I couldn't be happier for you!'

CHAPTER 24

EURO 2020: WEMBLEY WARRIORS

The last few years at Liverpool had been a special kind of run for Jordan – and he still got a jolt of pride when he looked at the medals and framed shirts from those unforgettable games. But now he wanted to repeat that kind of success with England.

'The last World Cup was a huge leap forward, but I know we can go one step further at the Euros,' he told Rebecca as he organised his clothes, chargers and iPad ready for the tournament.

'Plus, the final is at Wembley,' Rebecca added, smiling. 'What a moment that would be for the whole country!'

The only downside was that Jordan was again

dealing with an injury. After surgery to repair a muscle in his thigh, the recovery timeline made it unlikely that he would be back for Euro 2020 (being played in 2021 due to the health crisis). But he had attacked the rehab with his usual commitment, and his reward was a place in Gareth's squad.

Still, Jordan knew he was playing catch-up. 'I've missed so much football since February,' he said to Andy Robertson, who would be at the tournament too with Scotland. 'If I can offer something off the bench, great. But Gareth has to go with the lads who are sharp.'

With Declan Rice and Kalvin Phillips starting in midfield, England made it through to a quarter-final against Germany. Jordan watched nervously from the bench as England won a tight battle with two goals in the last fifteen minutes. After the second goal, Gareth signalled for Jordan to get ready to come on for the final few minutes. As he jogged on, it felt good to be part of a historic moment, even briefly.

In the quarter-final against Ukraine, Jordan got more game-time, and that wasn't all. With England already winning 3–0, Southgate sent him on to keep things tight in midfield, but he had the energy to get forward too. In the sixty-third minute, Mason Mount curled a corner into the middle and Jordan burst into the six-yard box, following it all the way. Then as the ball dropped, he jumped up and powered a glancing header into the bottom corner. *4–0!*

Goooooooooooooooooooaaaaaaaaaaaaaaaalllllllllllllllllllllllllll!!!!!!!!!!!!!!!!!!!!

'Get in!' Jordan roared, punching the air with real passion and pride. In his sixty-second international appearance, he had finally scored his first goal for England, and it was a feeling that he would never, ever forget.

Jordan was back on the bench for the semi-final against Denmark, but Southgate brought him on in extra-time with the score tied at 1–1. The Danes were exhausted and Jordan quickly took control in midfield, sparking England attacks and getting forward down the right wing.

'Let's go, lads,' he shouted. 'We just need one chance!'

With a mazy run, Raheem created that chance. He went down in the box and the referee pointed to the spot. Harry did the rest. His penalty was saved but the ball rebounded to him for a simple finish.

England were into the final!

'Just the big one left now!' Jordan shouted to Harry as they took a quick lap around Wembley.

Harry grinned. 'Yeah, I can't wait for that! Look at all the happy faces in the crowd. It means so much to them, particularly after what everyone has been through over the last year.'

Gareth gathered the squad for a string of meetings leading up to the final, laying out the tactics and keeping the mood light. The Euro 2020 final against Italy was all anyone wanted to talk about.

Jordan would be on the bench again for the final, but he hoped his body would hold up for another thirty minutes or more if Gareth called on him. England got off to a flying start, with Luke Shaw firing home a shot off the inside of the post within two minutes.

But Italy scrapped their way back into the game and pulled level. Jordan could feel the momentum shifting and he wasn't surprised when Gareth gave him the signal that he was coming on. He tried to settle things down in midfield with short, simple passes, but no-one could break the stalemate. As the minutes ticked down in extra time, Jordan was subbed off to allow Marcus Rashford to come on and take a penalty. Now all he could do was cross his fingers and hope.

The shootout was a heartbreaker. After a strong start, Marcus's penalty hit the post and then Jadon and Bukayo both had their spot-kicks saved. It was all over and Italy, not England, would be lifting the Euro 2020 trophy.

Despite his own disappointment, Jordan rushed straight over to comfort Marcus, Jadon and Bukayo. After all, he knew what it felt like to miss a penalty in a major tournament. He had been spared the backlash because England had gone through against Colombia, but he could imagine the pain that these young players were experiencing. He knew they would all bounce back, but it was tough to get that message across to them when everything was still so raw.

As he parked in his driveway that night, Jordan

took a deep breath. If things had gone differently, the England players would have been parading around with the trophy and preparing to party late into the night. This time, it just wasn't meant to be, but together the team had made their country proud. From the World Cup semi-finals in 2018, they had gone on to reach the Euro final in 2021 – that was real progress.

When he went inside his house, Rebecca and the kids rushed to wrap him in hugs, washing away the pain. With family time to come and another exciting season ahead with Liverpool, there was no time to dwell on missed opportunities. 'Thanks!' he said. 'I needed that.'

Settling down to enjoy the rest of the summer break, Jordan thought back over the past ten years and his journey from Sunderland youngster to England international to Liverpool captain to Champions League and Premier League winner – and everything in between. He had needed every ounce of determination along the way, but his dreams had come true.

Plus, there were still plenty of chapters left to be written. Jordan tied his shoelaces and set off for a morning run. The next big game would be here in no time at all.

JORDAN HENDERSON HONOURS

Liverpool

- League Cup: 2011–12, 2021-22
- UEFA Champions League: 2018–19
- UEFA Super Cup: 2019
- FIFA Club World Cup: 2019
- Premier League: 2019–20
- FA Community Shield: 2022
- FA Cup: 2022

Individual

- Sunderland Young Player of the Year: 2009–10, 2010–11

- 🏆 Liverpool Young Player of the Year: 2011–12
- 🏆 England U21 Player of the Year Award: 2012
- 🏆 England Senior Men's Player of the Year: 2019
- 🏆 FWA Footballer of the Year: 2019–20
- 🏆 Liverpool Fans' Player of the Season Award: 2019–20
- 🏆 PFA Premier League Team of the Year: 2019–20

HENDERSON

14 THE FACTS

NAME: Jordan Brian Henderson

DATE OF BIRTH: 17 June 1990

PLACE OF BIRTH: Sunderland

NATIONALITY: English

BEST FRIEND: Adam Lallana

CURRENT CLUB: Liverpool

POSITION: CDM

THE STATS

Height (cm):	182
Club appearances:	557
Club goals:	39
Club assists:	72
Club trophies:	8
International appearances:	73
International goals:	3
International trophies:	0
Ballon d'Ors:	0

★ ★ ★ **HERO RATING: 87** ★ ★ ★

GREATEST MOMENTS

 **19 DECEMBER 2009,
MANCHESTER CITY 4–3 SUNDERLAND**

Although his team ended up losing the match,
Jordan must have been delighted with this midfield
masterclass. Against the Premier League's new richest
club, he fired in his first ever Premier League goal
and then set up another for Kenwyne Jones with
an incredible cross. What a young superstar!

16 SEPTEMBER 2016, CHELSEA 1–2 LIVERPOOL

In Jordan's sixth season at Liverpool, the club was entering an exciting new era under manager Jürgen Klopp. In this game, they showed their potential by beating Chelsea at Stamford Bridge, and who scored an absolute worldie of a winning goal? Jordan, Liverpool's new leader! From 25 yards out, he took one touch to cushion the ball before whipping an unstoppable, dipping strike into the top corner.

1 JUNE 2019, LIVERPOOL 2–0 TOTTENHAM

Their second Champions League final in two years, but this time Jordan led his Liverpool team to victory. Yes, they were European Champions at last! Although he didn't score or set up a goal, Jordan played an important part all over the pitch, and after lifting the trophy, he enjoyed an emotional celebration with his proud father.

22 JULY 2020, LIVERPOOL 5–3 CHELSEA

After thirty years of failure and disappointment, this was the day when Liverpool were finally crowned Premier League Champions for the very first time! It was a massive moment for the club, even though sadly no fans were allowed at Anfield due to COVID-19. Jordan was injured for the game itself, but he was there at the end to lift the trophy as Liverpool's inspirational captain.

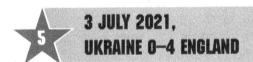

3 JULY 2021, UKRAINE 0–4 ENGLAND

When Jordan came on in this Euro 2020 quarter-final, England were already cruising to victory, but there was still time for a very proud personal moment. From Mason Mount's corner, Jordan jumped up and headed the ball home to get his first England goal. What an achievement – it had only taken him sixty-two games to score it!

PLAY LIKE YOUR HEROES

A JORDAN HENDERSON
MIDFIELD MASTERCLASS

STEP 1: Every football match is a battle that you're determined to win. That's your mindset, from kick-off all the way through to the final whistle.

STEP 2: When the other team have the ball, don't stop running and working until you win it back. Tackle, press, block, intercept – with your energy, you're everywhere on the pitch.

STEP 3: As well as an important player, you're also a leader. So, use your voice to communicate with your teammates, encouraging and organising them.

STEP 4: Once you've won the ball back for your team, it's time to attack. Skill and speed aren't necessarily your greatest strengths, so move the ball forward to your strikers as quickly as possible. Sometimes, a short, simple pass will be the best option, but your long diagonal balls are also really dangerous.

STEP 5: Once you've passed the ball on, keep running into the opposition box. Okay, so the strikers are more likely to score, but you never know when a rebound might fall to you.

STEP 6: *GOAL!* Even if you haven't scored it, you're always at the centre of all celebrations. Football is a big team effort and the fans love to see your passion.

STEP 7: Once the celebrations are over, however, it's straight back to the battle. Run, tackle; run, press; run, block; run, intercept – yes, you'll do anything to lead your team to victory.

TEST YOUR KNOWLEDGE

QUESTIONS

1. What gift did Jordan's dad buy for him, well before his first birthday?

2. When Jordan was playing for Sunderland Under 11s, which first-team stars did he have a kickaround with?

3. As a Sunderland youth player, Jordan showed off his skills on which famous football TV show?

4. Which Sunderland manager handed Jordan his Premier League debut?

5. Which Sunderland manager made Jordan a regular starter during the 2009–10 season?

6. On his England debut in 2010, Jordan played alongside which two future Liverpool teammates in midfield?

7. When Liverpool finished second in 2014, why did Jordan miss their important Premier League matches against Chelsea and Crystal Palace?

8. Who did Jordan replace as Liverpool captain in 2015?

9. Jordan scored a penalty for England at the 2018 World Cup – true or false?

10. What did Jordan do to help people in need during the coronavirus pandemic?

11. Who set up Jordan's first ever England goal against Ukraine at Euro 2020?

Players Together charitable fund. **11.** *Mason Mount*
10. *He supported the North Liverpool Foodbank and helped create the*
9. *False – His spot-kick was saved in the shootout against Colombia.*
7. *He got sent off against Manchester City.* **8.** *Stevie Gerrard.*
5. *Steve Bruce.* **6.** *Stevie Gerrard and James Milner.*
2. *Strikers Niall Quinn and Kevin Phillips.* **3.** *Soccer AM.* **4.** *Roy Keane.*
1. *His first Sunderland Football Club shirt!*

172

CAN'T GET ENOUGH OF
ULTIMATE FOOTBALL HEROES?

Check out heroesfootball.com
for quizzes, games, and competitions!

Plus join the Ultimate Football Heroes
Fan Club to score exclusive content
and be the first to hear about
new books and events.
heroesfootball.com/subscribe/